Woodstock Ontario Book 1 in Colour Photos, Saving Our History One Photo at a Time

Photography
by Barbara Raué
2015

Series Name:
Cruising Ontario

Book 125: Woodstock Book 1

Cover photo: Holstein Cow

Series Name: Cruising Ontario
Saving Our History One Photo at a Time
in colour photos

Books Available in Alphabetical Order:
Aberfoyle, Acton, Alton, Ancaster, Arthur, Aylmer, Ayr, Bloomingdale, Brantford, Burlington, Caledon, Caledonia, Cambridge, Clifford, Conestogo, Delhi, Dorchester to Aylmer, Drayton, Drumbo, Dundas, Eden Mills, Elmira, Elora, Fergus, Guelph, Hagersville, Hamilton, Hanover, Harriston, Hespeler, Jarvis, Kitchener, Linwood, Listowel, London, Lucknow, Mono, Mount Forest, Neustadt, New Hamburg, Niagara-on-the-Lake, Oakville, Orangeville, Orillia, Owen Sound, Palmerston, Peterborough, Port Elgin, Preston, Rockwood, Seaforth, Sheffield, Shelburne, Simcoe, Southampton, St. Jacobs, St. Thomas, Stoney Creek, Stratford, Tillsonburg, Waterdown, Waterford, Waterloo, Wellesley, Wingham

Book 110:Lucknow, Mitchell
Book 111: Conestogo, Bloomingdale
Book 112: Delhi
Book 113: Waterford
Book 114-116: Waterloo
Book 117-119: Windsor
Book 120-121: Amherstburg
Book 122: Essex
Book 123-124: Kingsville & Area
Book 125-126: Woodstock

Other Books by Barbara Raue

Coins of Gold

Arrows, Indians and Love

The Life and Times of Barbara
Volume 1: Inventions That Have Enhanced My Life
Volume 2: Entertainment That I Have Enjoyed
Volume 3: East Coast Trips
Volume 4: Olympics Have Always Intrigued Me
Volume 5: Wonders of the World
Volume 6: Caribbean Cruises We Have Enjoyed
Volume 7: Animals
Volume 8: Storms and Other Major Disasters in My Lifetime
Volume 9: Wars, Terrorist Attacks and Major Disasters

The Cromwell Family Book

Laura Secord Discovered

Daddy Where Are You?

Visit Barbara's website to view all of her books
http://barbararaue.ca

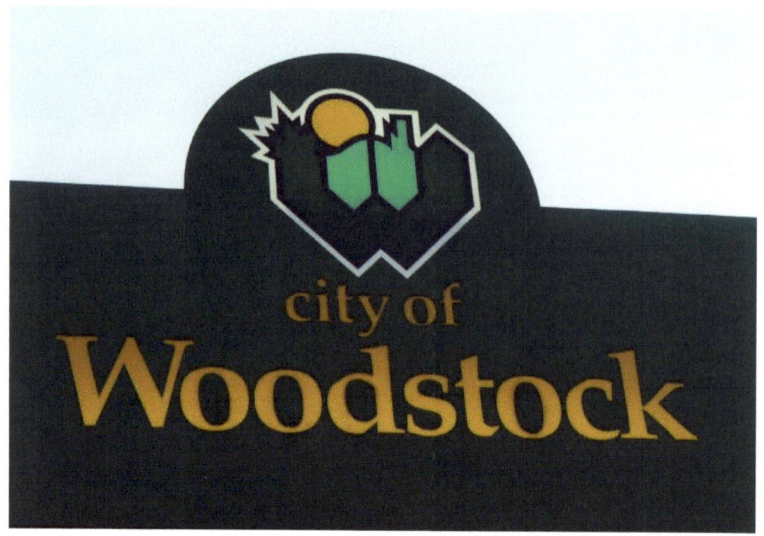

Woodstock is located in the heart of South Western Ontario, at the junction of highways 401 and 403, 50 km east of London and 60 km west of Kitchener. Woodstock is the largest municipality in Oxford County, a county known for its rich farmland, and for its dairy and cash crop farming. As well as being "The Dairy Capital of Canada", Woodstock also has a large industrial base, much of which is related to the auto manufacturing industry.

In 1792, Sir John Graves Simcoe became Lieutenant Governor of Upper Canada and made plans for the development of the interior of Upper Canada. He envisioned a series of town sites linked by a military road and a system of rivers and canals, providing inland access during an era when commerce and settlements depended on major waterways. London, Chatham, Dorchester and Oxford were designated town sites with London as the defensible capital. The military road stretching from Burlington Bay through Woodstock to London provided an overland supply route for the safe movement of troops and settlers. Simcoe named this road Dundas Street after Henry Dundas, Viscount Melville, Secretary of State for War and the Colonies.

To speed development in the sparsely populated interior of the province, Simcoe granted whole townships to land companies who were obligated to bring in settlers.

Simcoe passed through the area now known as Woodstock and noted it a suitable "Town Plot" and settlement began here in 1800.

In the 1830s, a different group of immigrants were encouraged to settle in Oxford to ensure this community's loyalty to the British crown. British naval and army officers placed on half-pay looked to the colonies for a new career at the conclusion of military service. The first to arrive was Alexander Whalley Light, a retired colonel who came to Oxford County in 1831. He was joined by Philip Graham in 1832, a retired captain of the Royal Navy, and Captain Andrew Drew, on half-pay from the Royal Navy, arrived in Woodstock to make preparations for his superior, Rear-Admiral Henry Vansittart, also on half-pay. Half-pay officers went to considerable lengths to clear their chosen parcels of land.

Admiral Vansittart commissioned Colonel Andrew Drew to build a church (Old St. Paul's) in a new area of Oxford that was known as the "Town Plot". The men later quarreled, which led to the construction of a second church known as "New St. Paul's".

Table of Contents

Wilson Street   Page 7

Dundas Street   Page 11

Reeve Street   Page 33

Peel Street   Page 35

Finkle Street   Page 35

Victoria Street   Page 36

Grace Street   Page 43

Buller Street   Page 45

Graham Street   Page 49

Adelaide Street   Page 52

Delatre Street   Page 53

Beale Street   Page 54

Architectural Terms   Page 55

Building Styles   Page 65

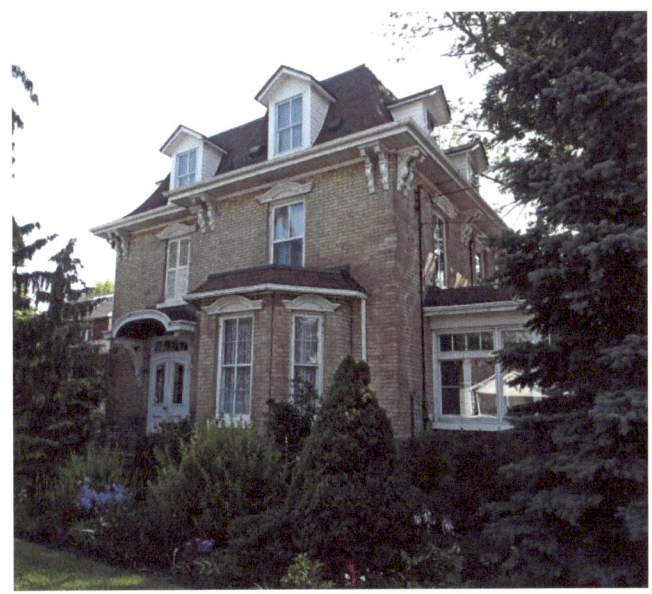

73 Wilson Street – Italianate/Second Empire – type of mansard roof with dormers, paired cornice brackets, bay window, window hoods

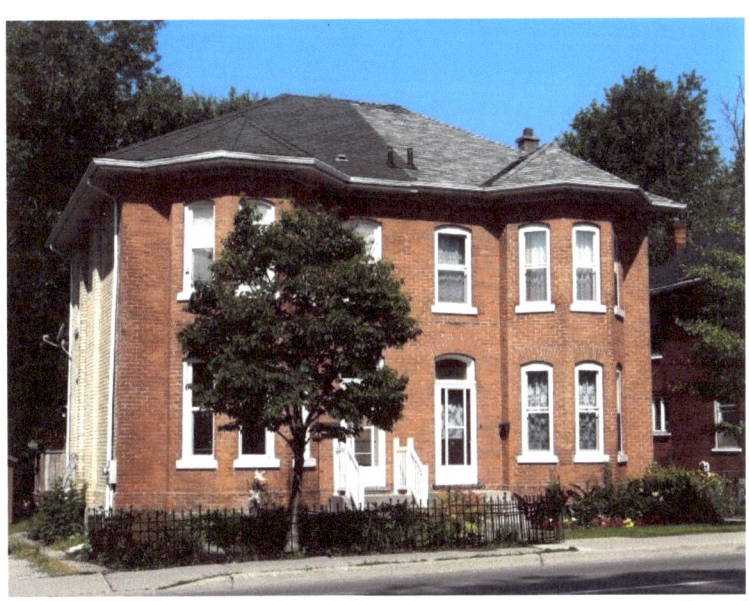

50-52 Wilson Street – hipped roof, two-storey tower-like bay

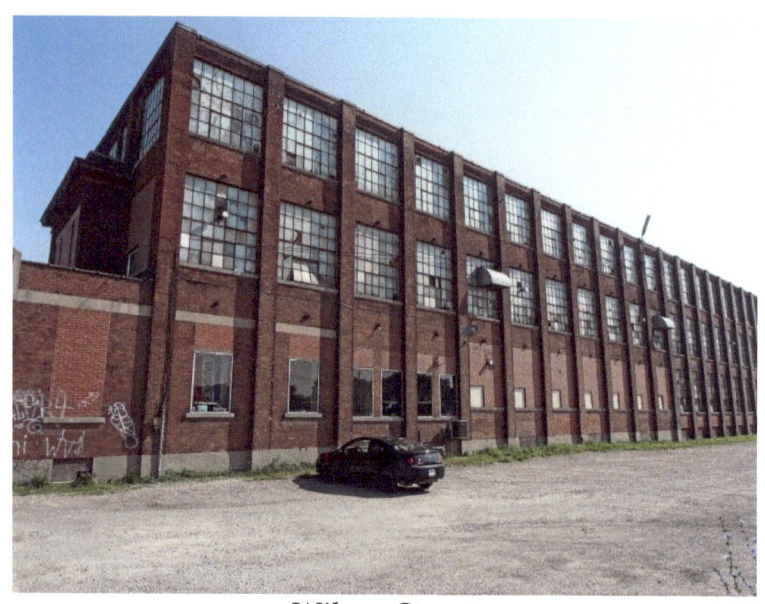

Wilson Street

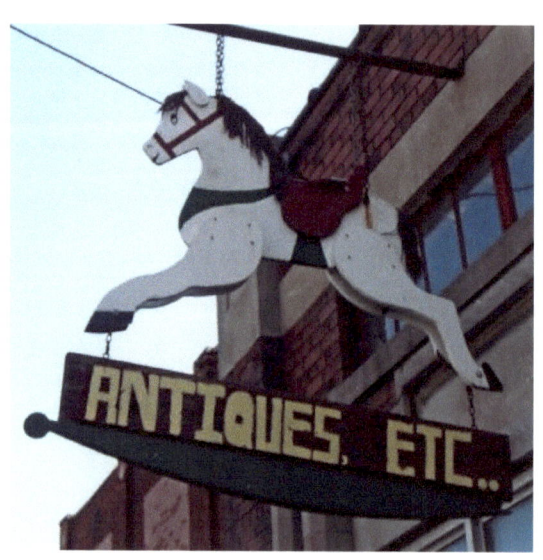

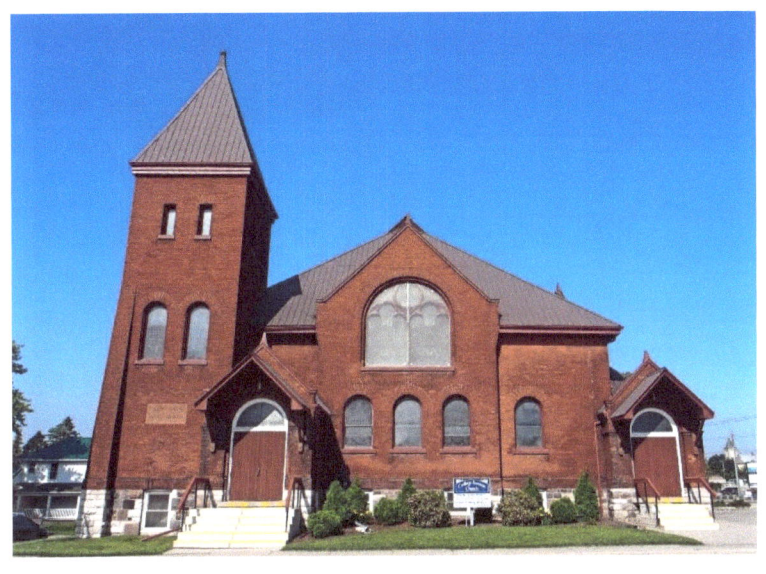

22 Wilson Street – College Avenue United Church - 1899

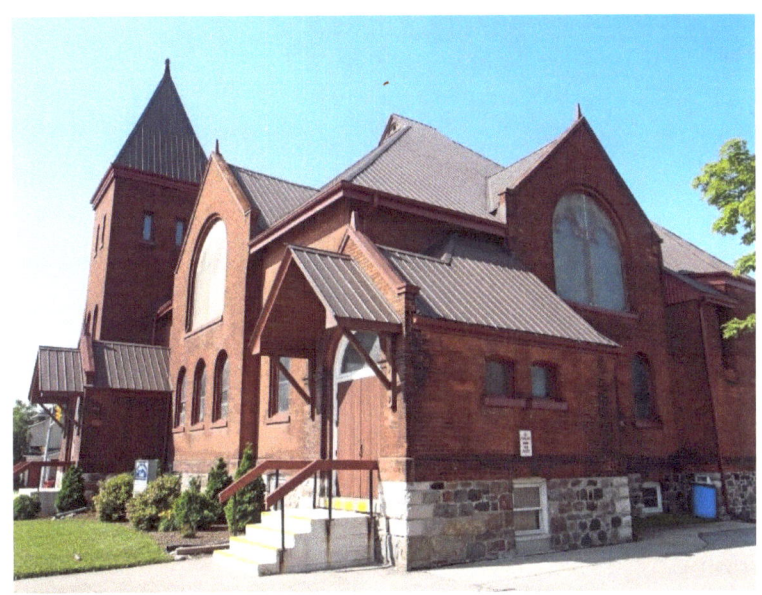

Cobblestone foundation

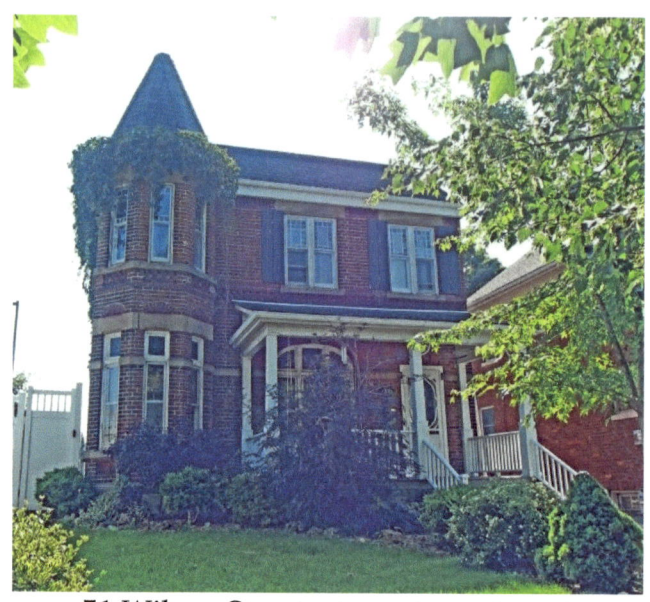

51 Wilson Street – two-storey turret

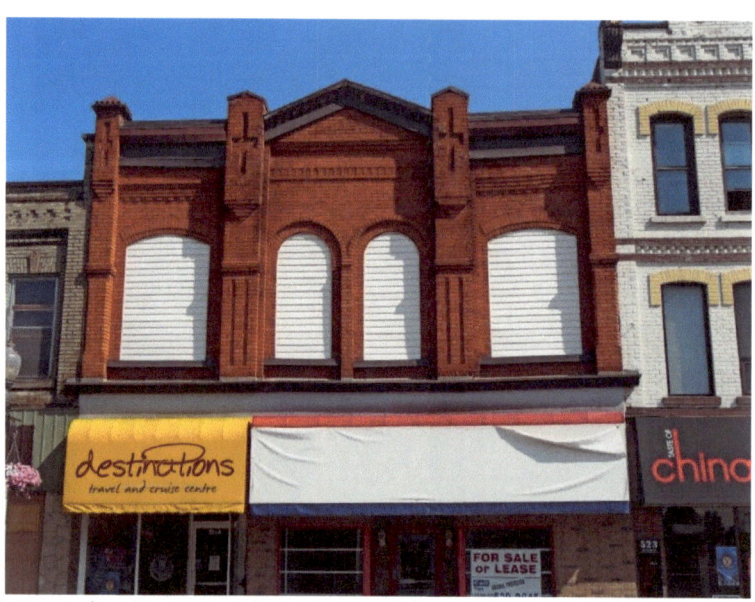

521 Dundas Street – dentil moulding, drip moulding around centre windows; reeded pilasters

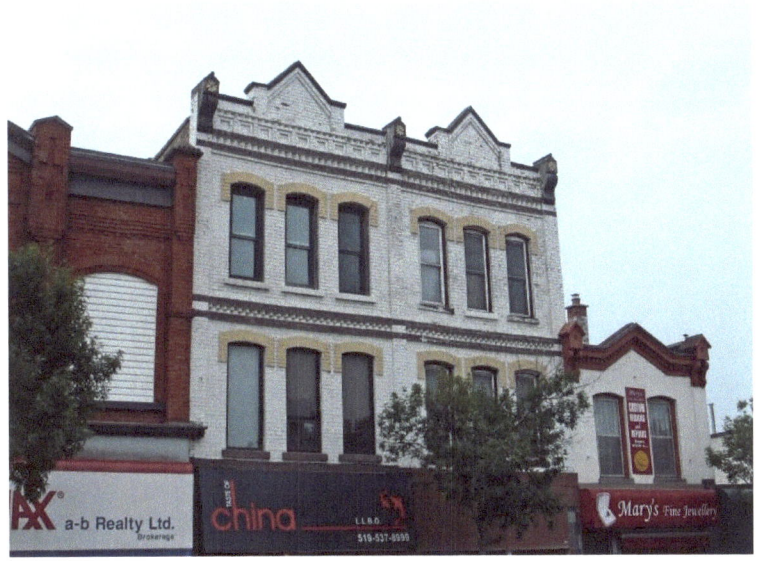

Dundas Street – saw tooth dentils with banding between storeys and above second storey, decorative brickwork, cornice brackets

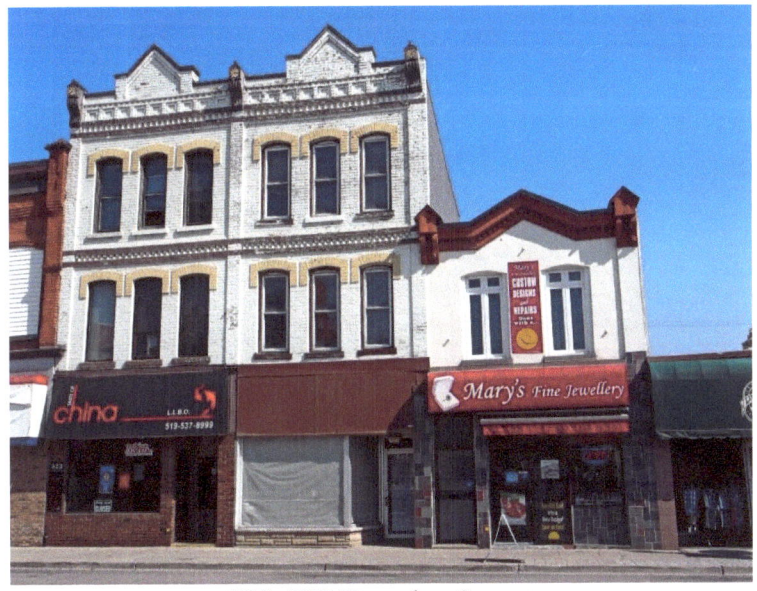

523-527 Dundas Street

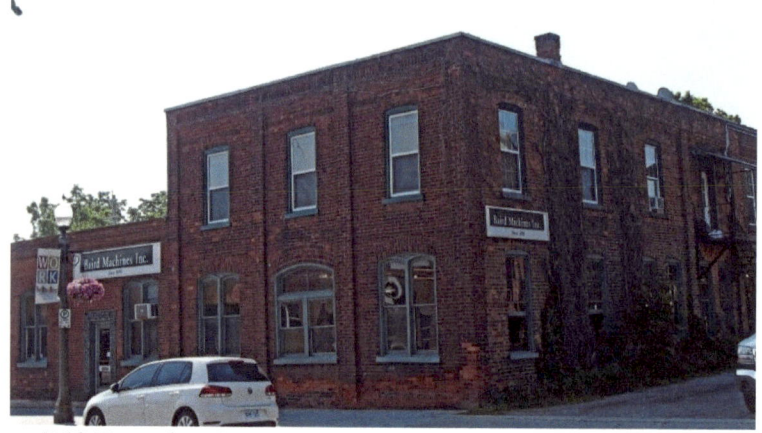

568 Dundas Street – Baird's Machine Shop c. 1900

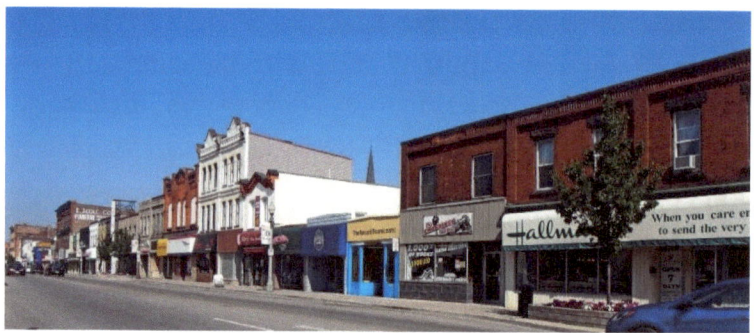

Dundas Street

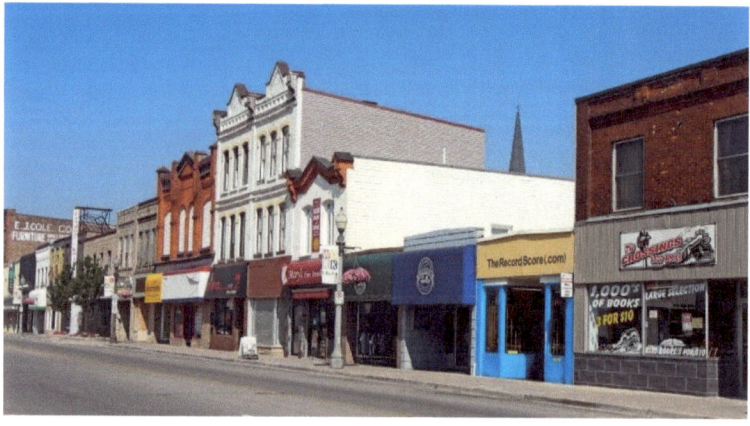

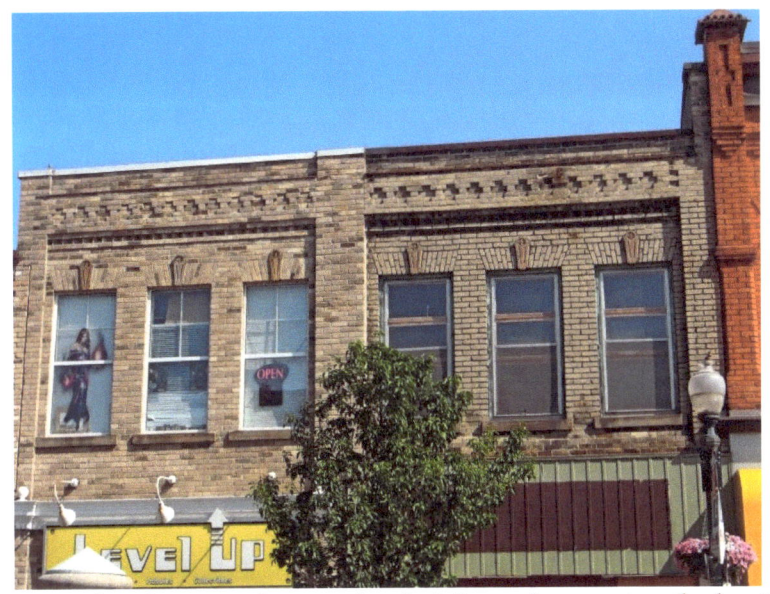

517 Dundas Street – decorative brickwork, saw tooth dentils, voussoirs with keystones

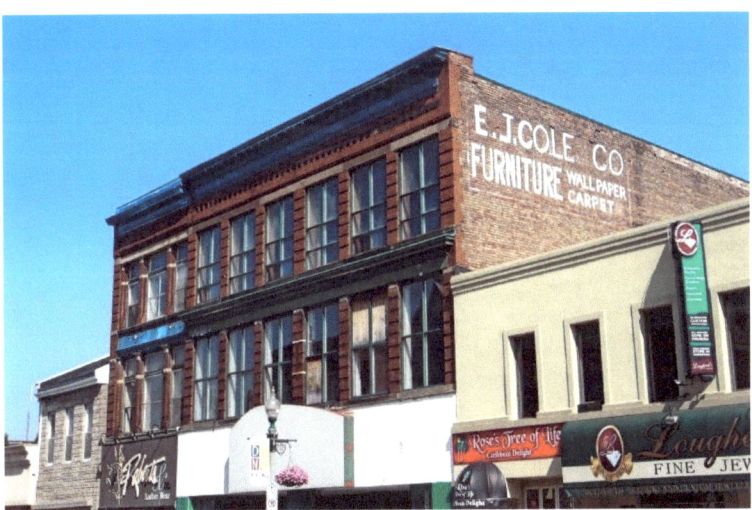

In 1902, E.J. Coles relocated his business to 493-494 Dundas, a large department store selling furniture, chinaware, hardware, floor coverings, draperies and a full line of groceries. In 1928, the business was sold to Canadian Department Stores, a subsidiary of T. Eaton Company.

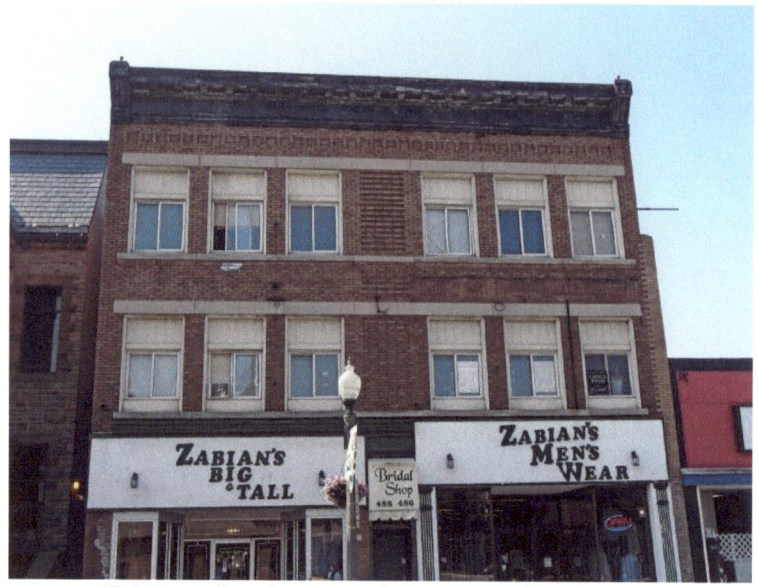

486 Dundas Street – decorative brickwork

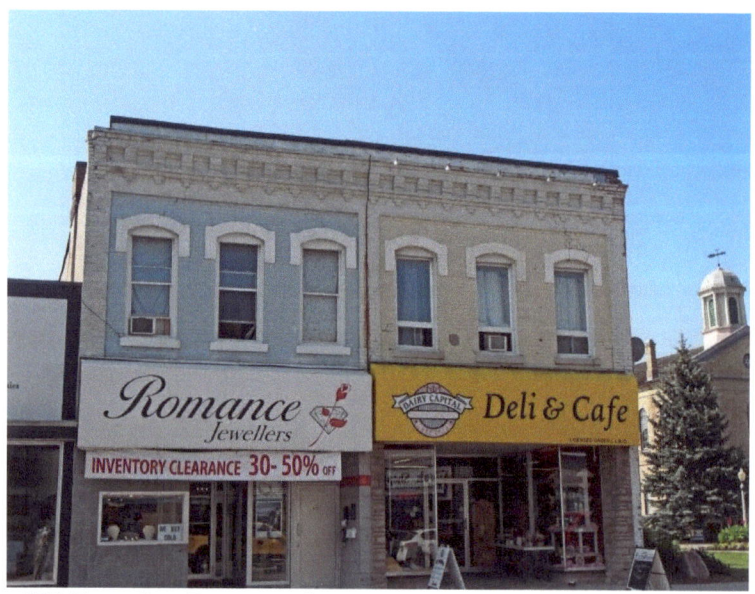

476 Dundas Street – decorative cornice with brackets

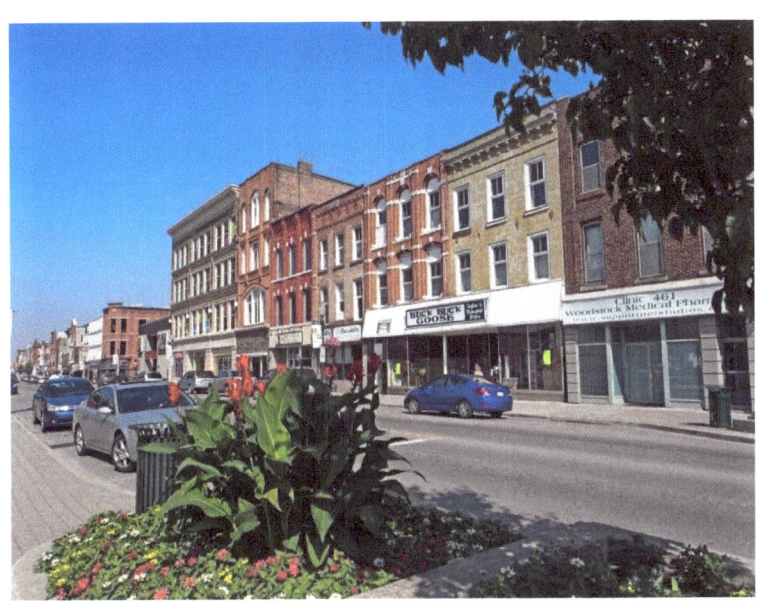

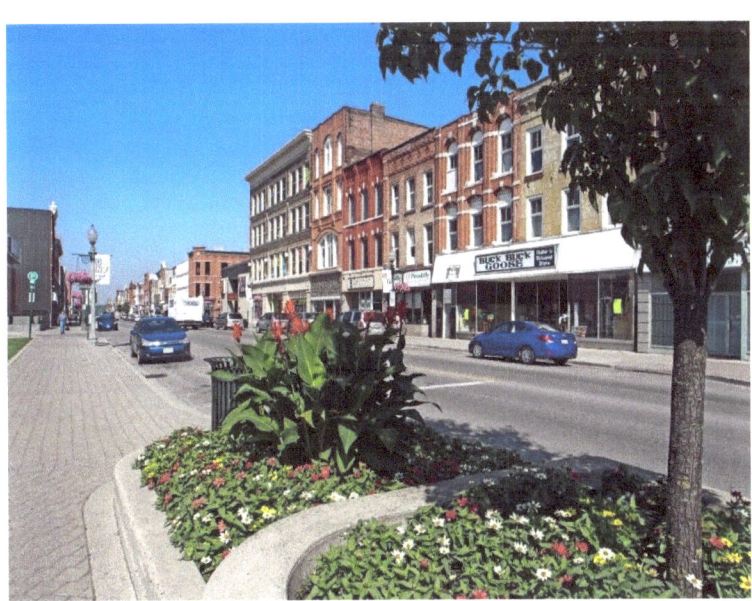

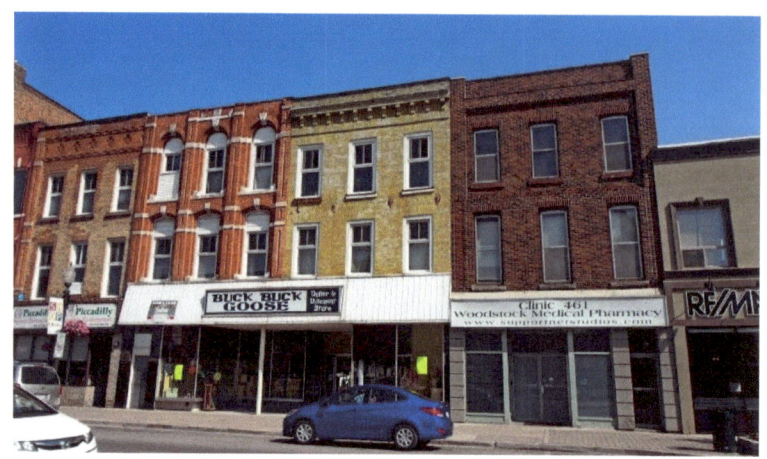

457 Dundas Street

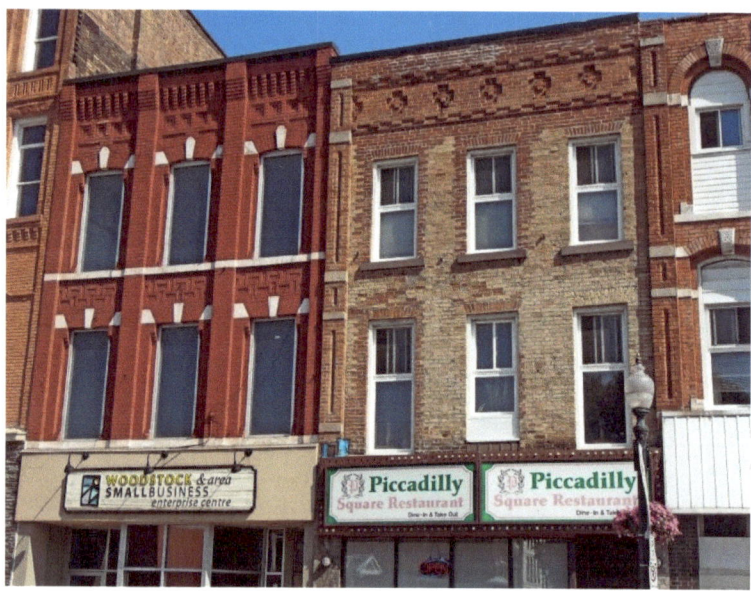

455 Dundas Street – pilasters, keystones, decorative brickwork

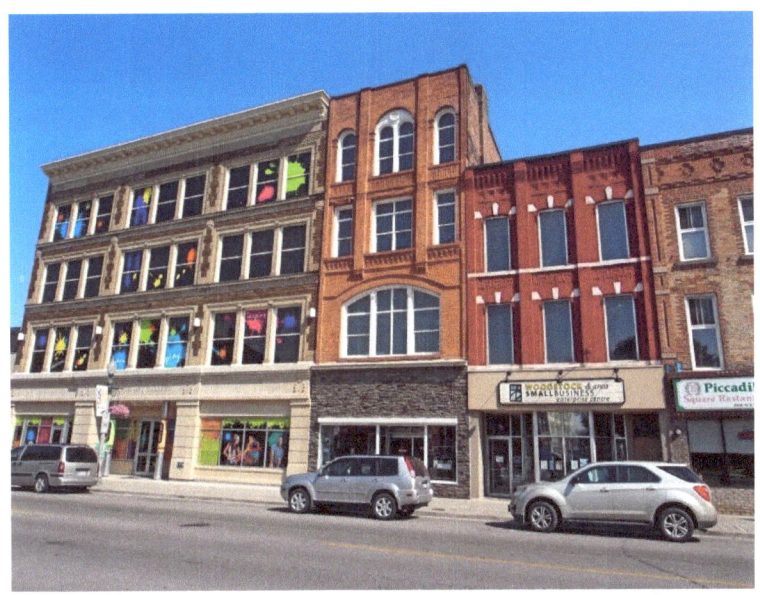

449 Dundas Street – dichromatic brickwork, lovely cornice

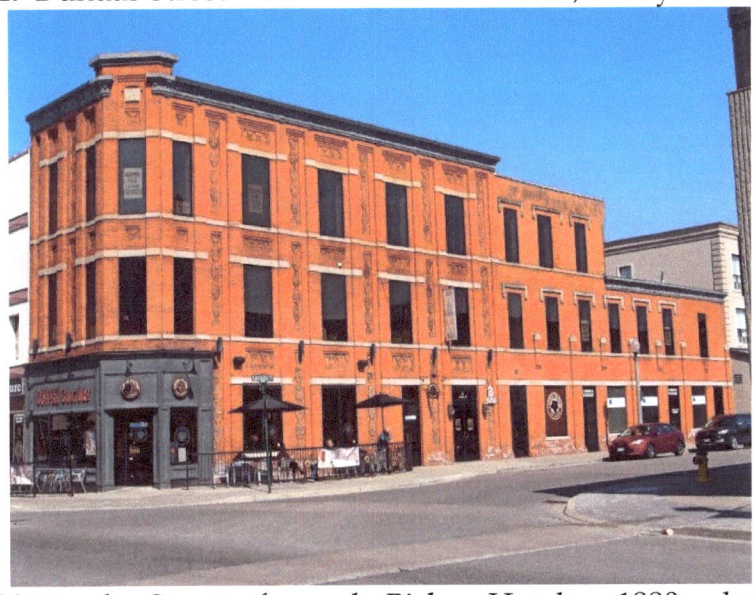

433 Dundas Street – formerly Bishop Hotel – c 1880s – later
operated by Samuel Woodroofe, Jeweller – detailed cornice,
the large "W" for Woodroofe and the dichromatic use of brick
in an X design

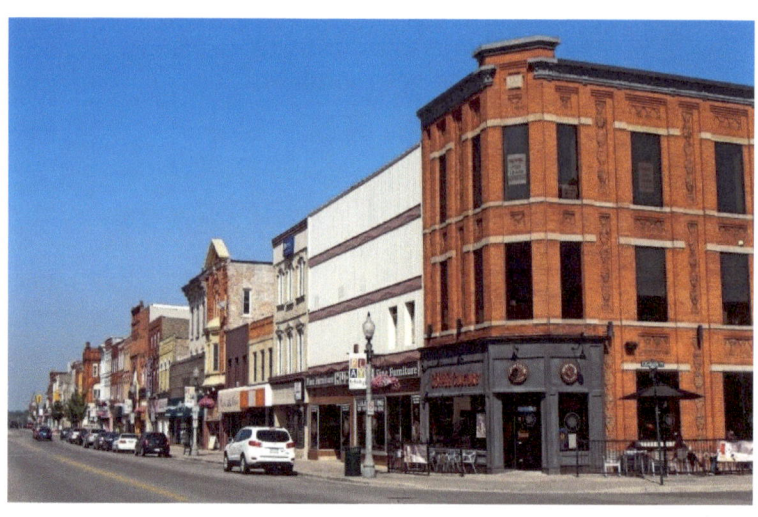

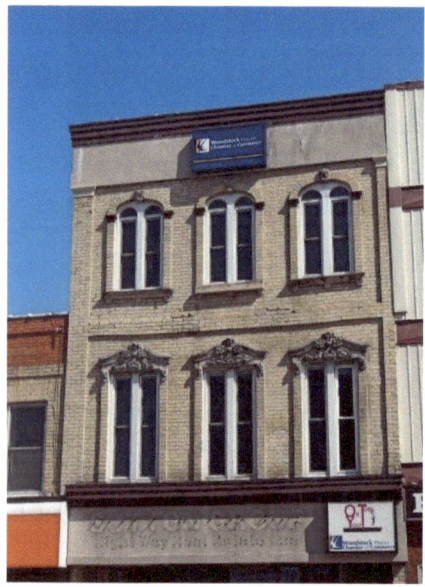
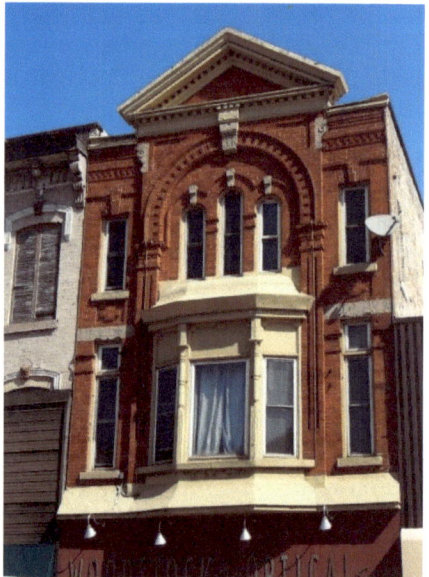

425 Dundas Street
voussoirs with keystones,
window hoods on lower floor

419 Dundas Street –
triangular pediment, dentils,
elaborate brickwork,
different style windows,
reeded pilaster and keystones

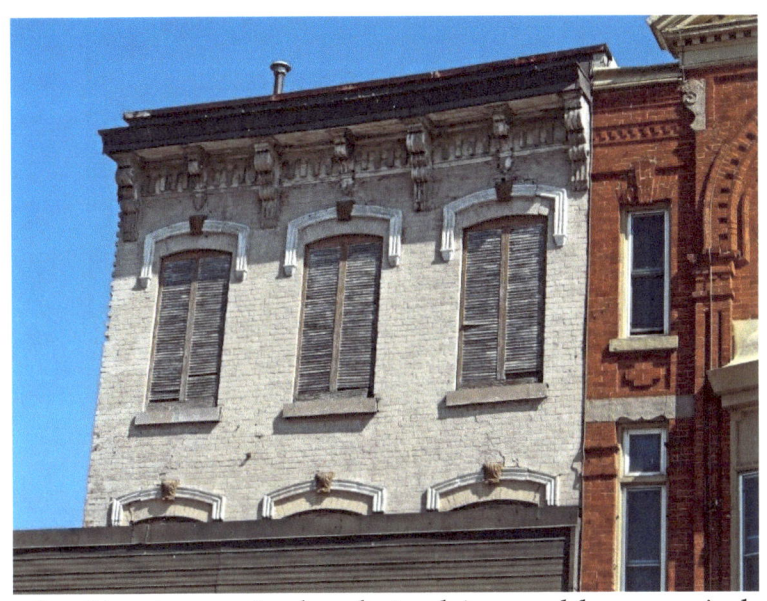

Dundas Street – cornice brackets, drip moulds over windows with keystones

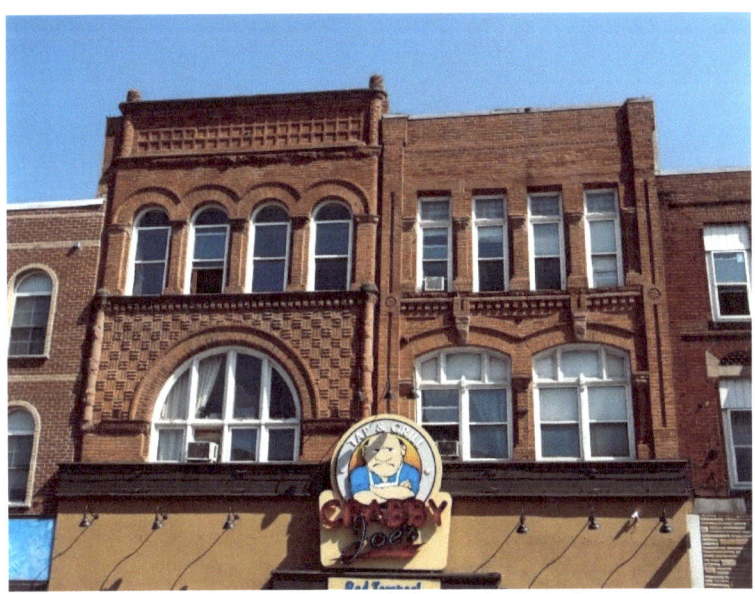

407-409 Dundas Street – beautiful semi-circular window with drip moulding and basket weave brickwork, terra cotta faces

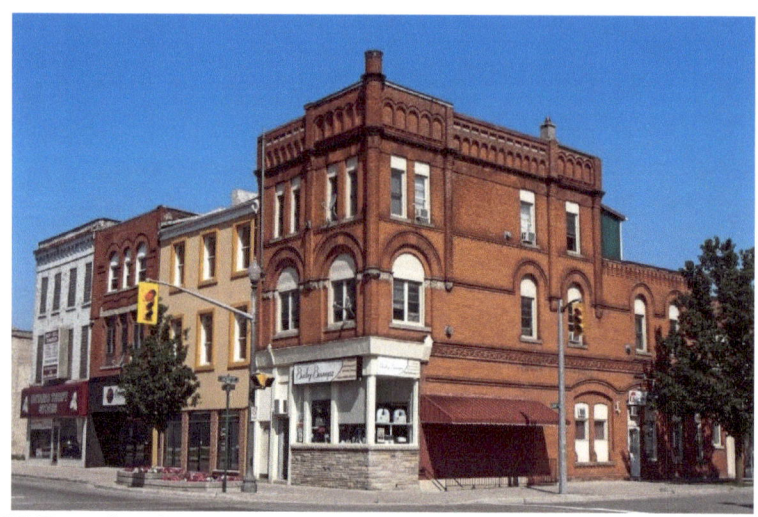

395 Dundas Street – turret, corbel brickwork, Romanesque style window arches, stringcourse of terra cotta in the rose design along Light Street

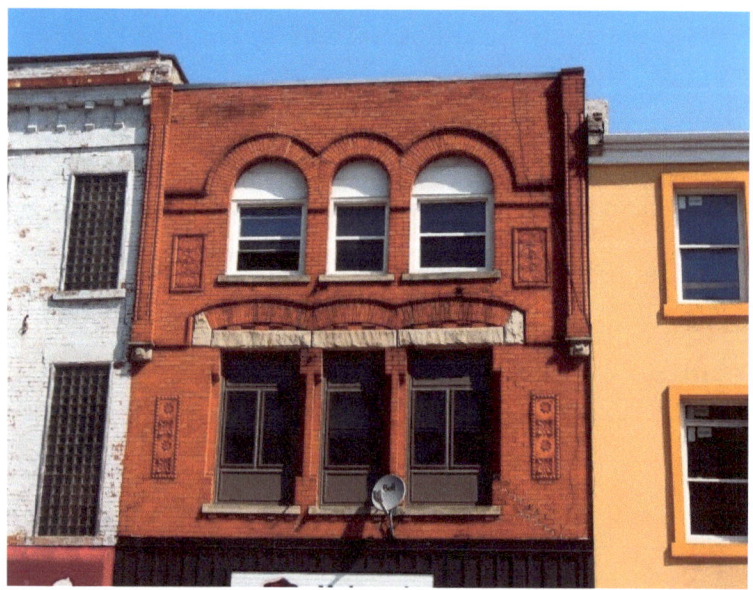

Decorative brickwork, pilasters

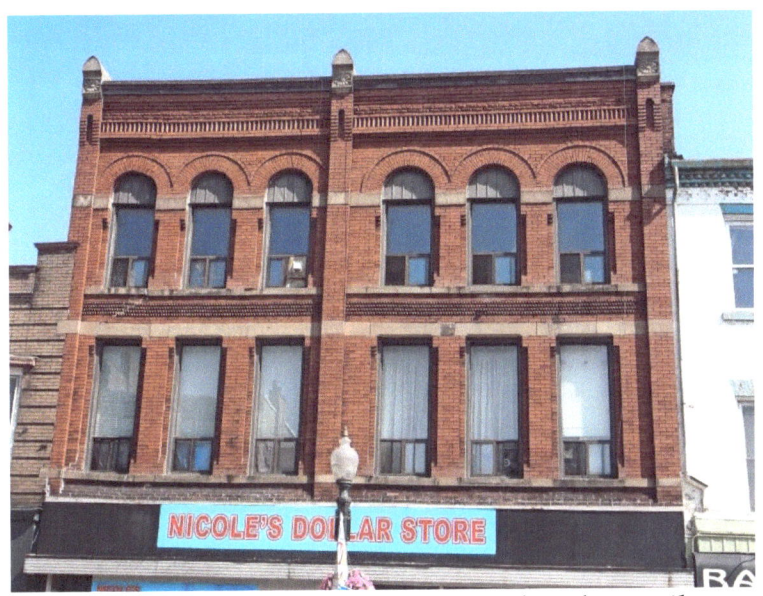

365 Dundas Street – dentil moulding, banding, pilasters

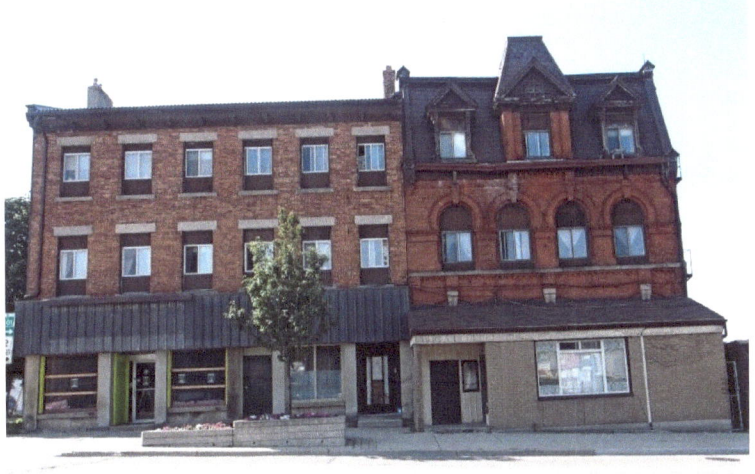

352-350 Dundas Street – Second Empire – central tower with fish scale shingles, dormers with supporting pilaster and brackets, china moon windows with brick drip moulding and keystones

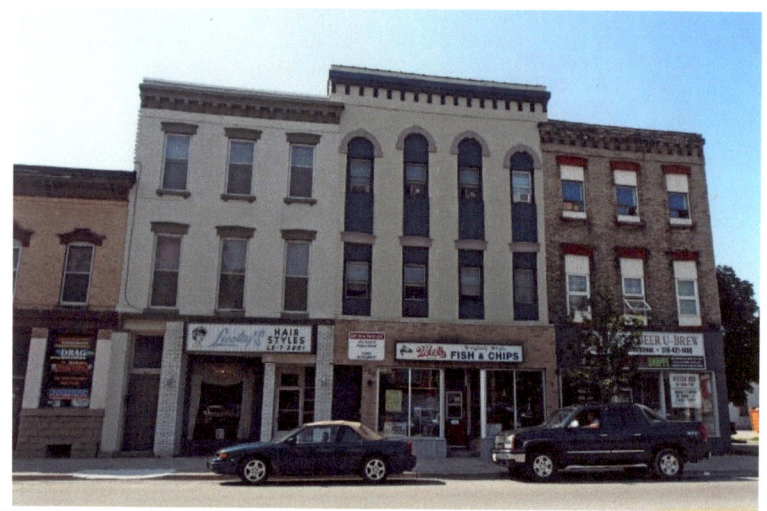

360-362 Dundas Street – window voussoirs with keystones, cornice brackets

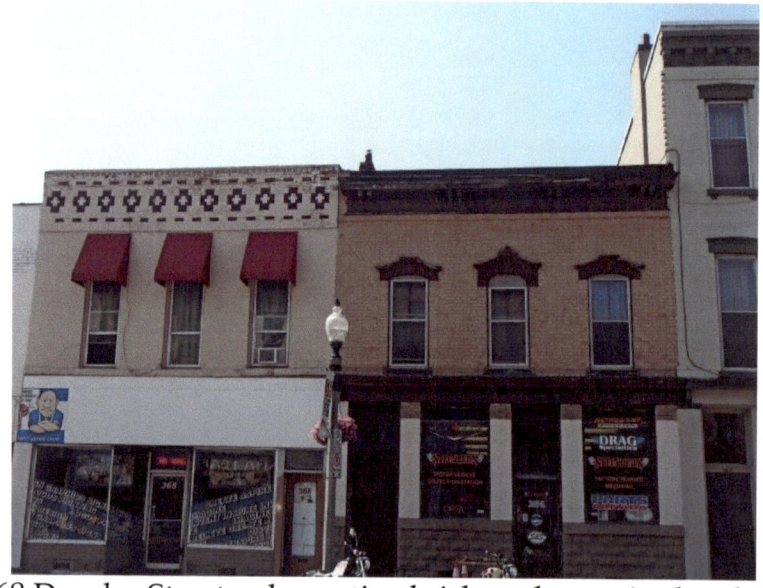

368 Dundas Street – decorative brickwork, cornice brackets

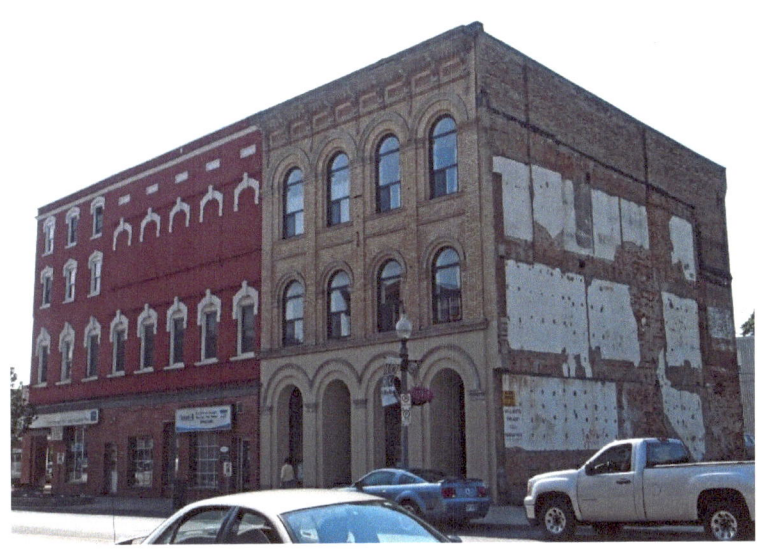

392 Dundas Street - pilasters, drip moulding over rounded windows, cornice brackets and dentil moulding

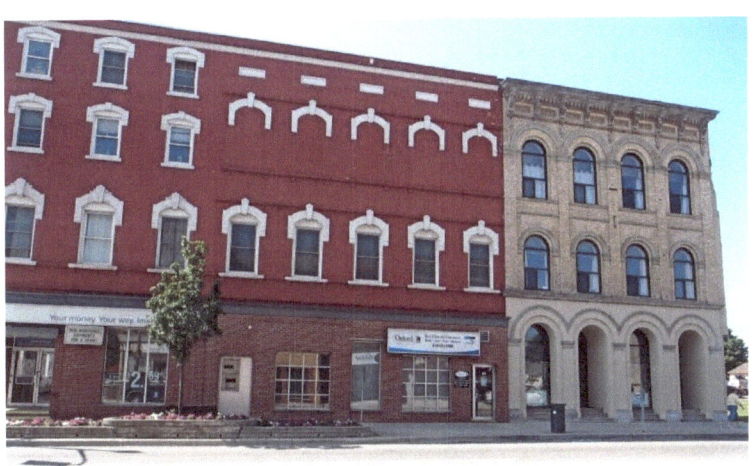

Voussoirs and keystones

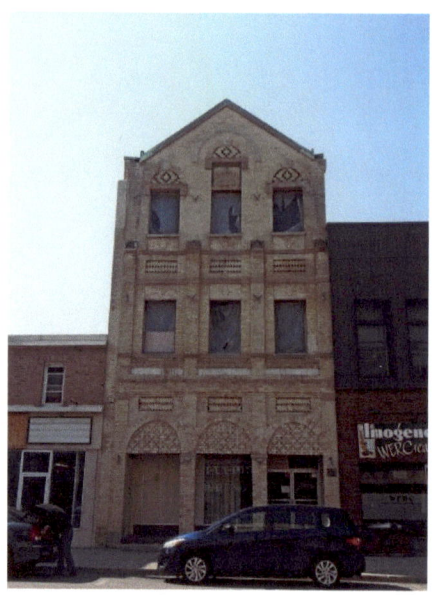

Decorative brickwork, pilasters

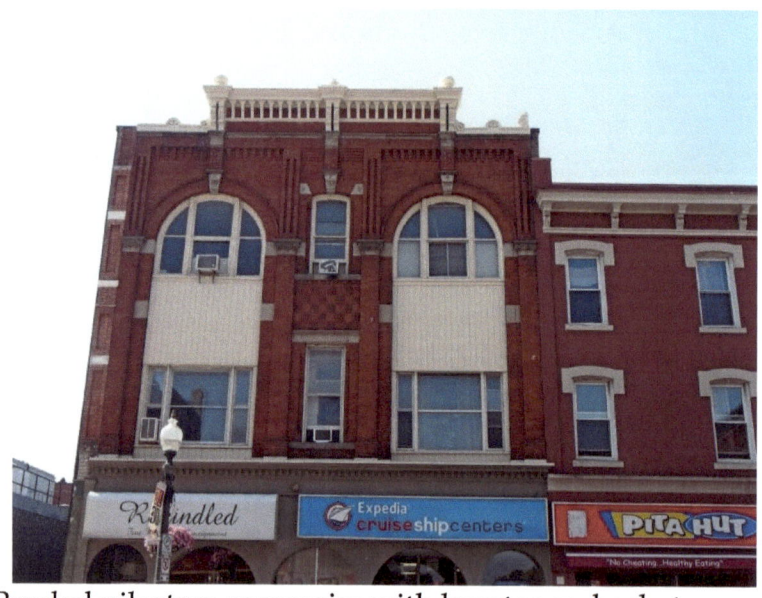

Reeded pilasters, voussoirs with keystones, basket weave
brickwork, bevelled dentil moulding on cornice

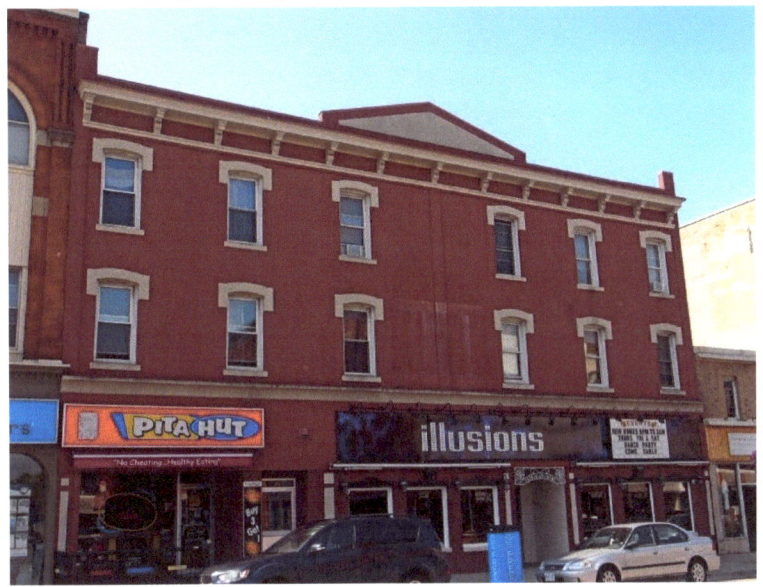

440 Dundas Street – cornice brackets

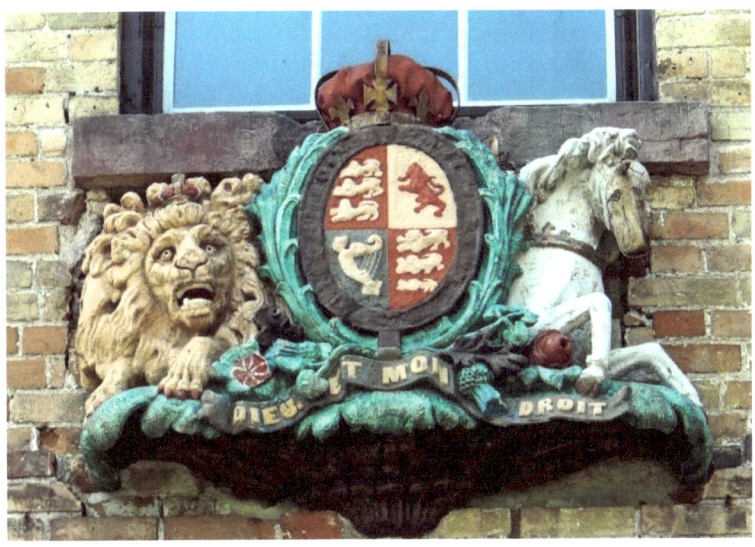

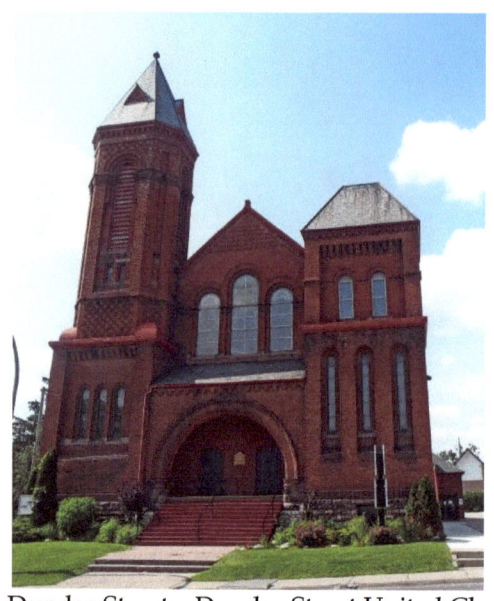

285 Dundas Street – Dundas Street United Church
Red brick, Romanesque-style

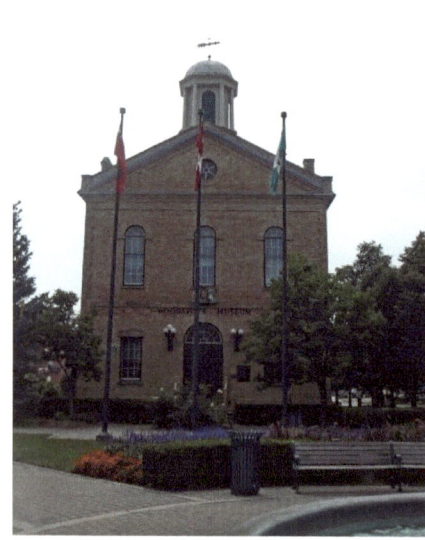

466 Dundas Street
– old Woodstock Town Hall
– now museum – 1853

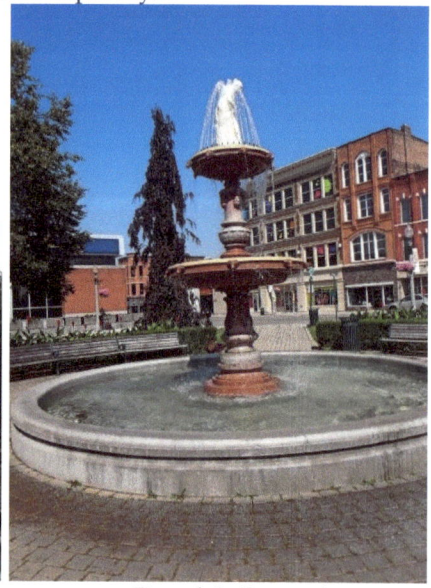

Pattulo's Fountain
erected in 1916 in honor of
Andrew Pattulo, head of the
Sentinel-Review newspaper in
early 20th century & Oxford MPP

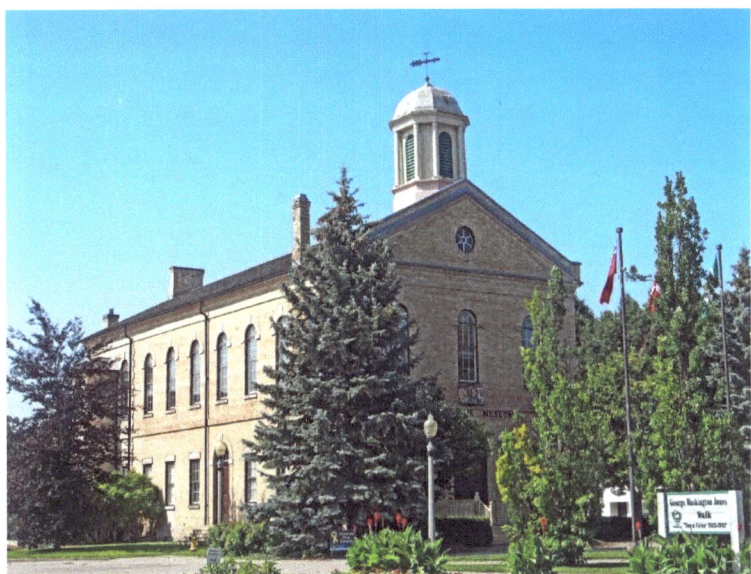

Cupola

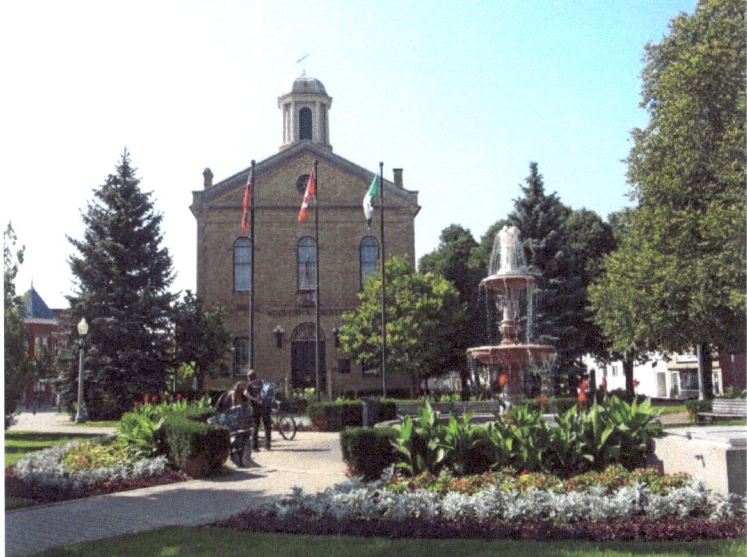

Patullo left a bequest of $1,000 to the City of Woodstock to purchase a fountain in his memory – cast iron, 16 feet, 8 inches high, topped by figure of woman pouring water from an urn

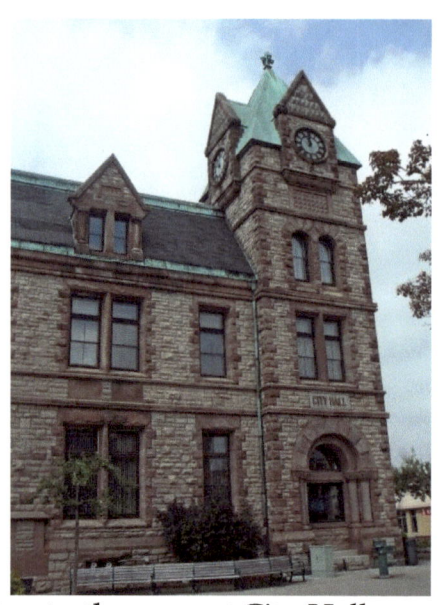

500 Dundas Street - the current City Hall was constructed of warm sandstone in 1899 as a post office; for over one hundred years it has been the centre of the municipal and social life of Woodstock. The corner tower has four clocks.

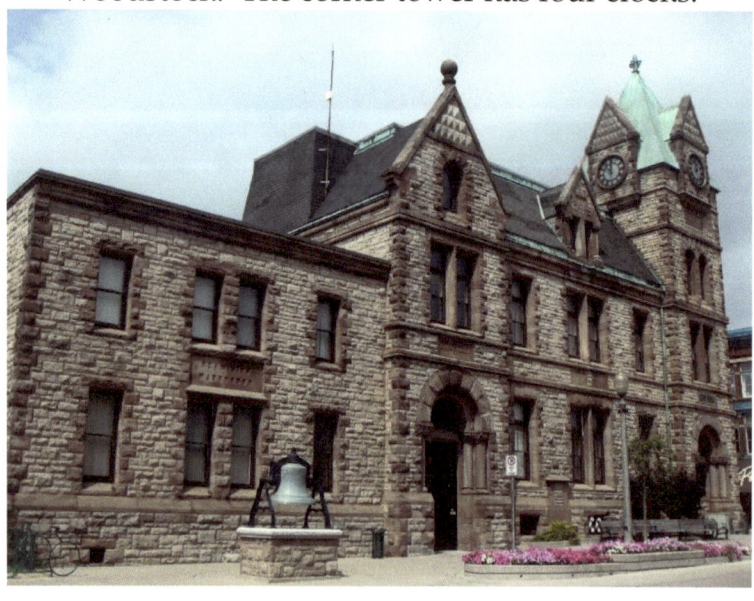

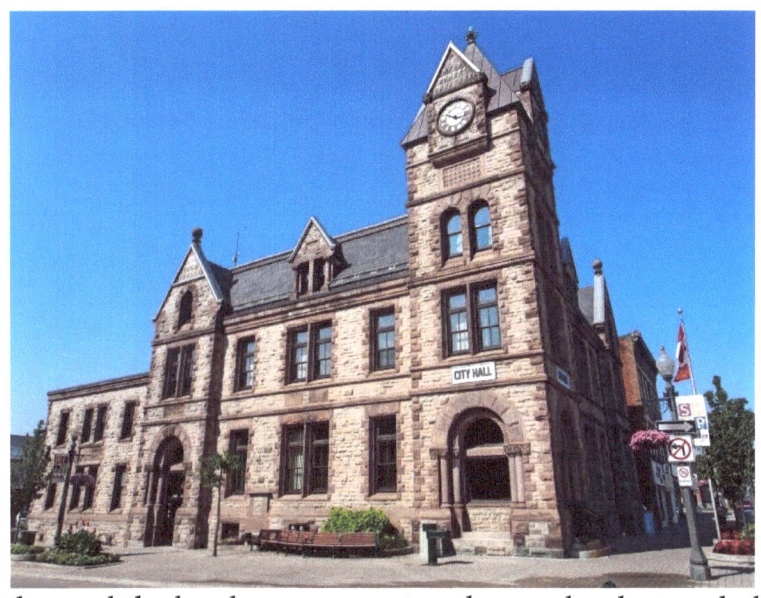

It housed the local government and served as lecture hall, opera house, and assize court. It is basically eighteenth century Palladian architecture.

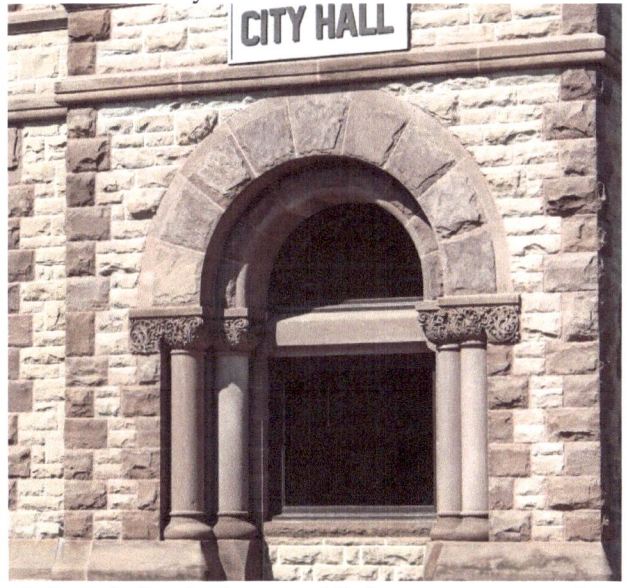

Round- headed windows with heavy surrounds reflect Italianate Revival

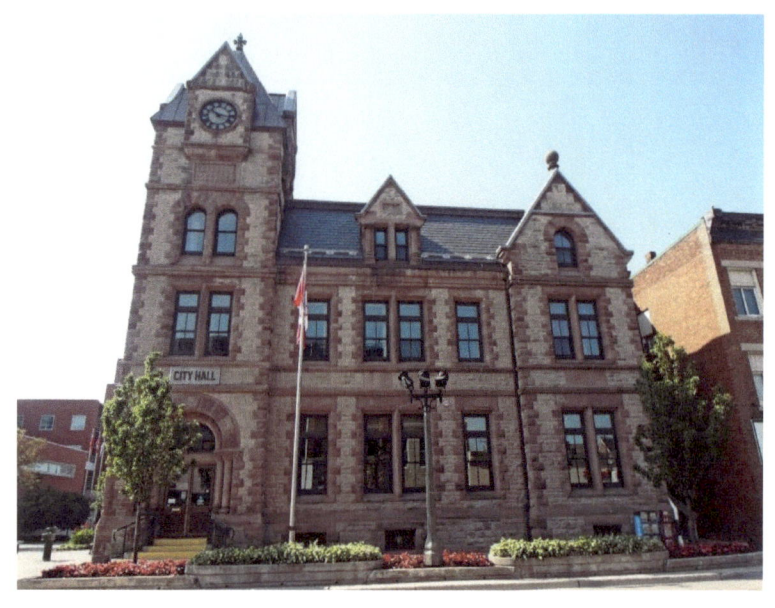

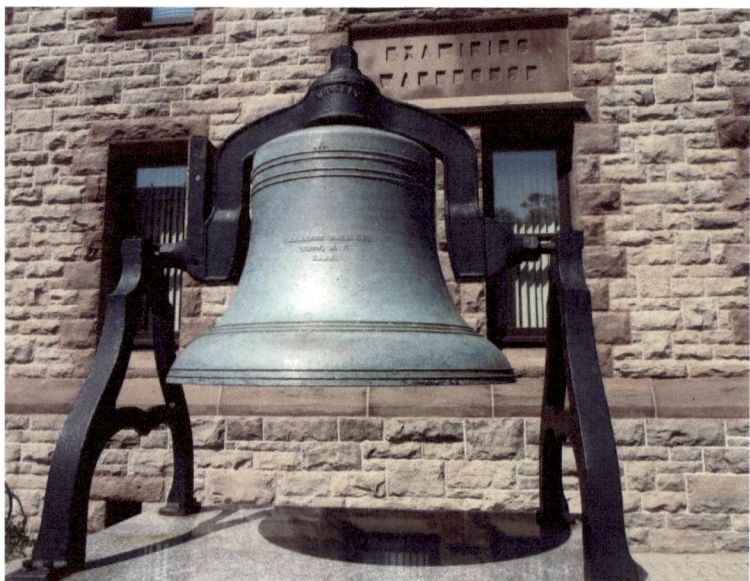

1902

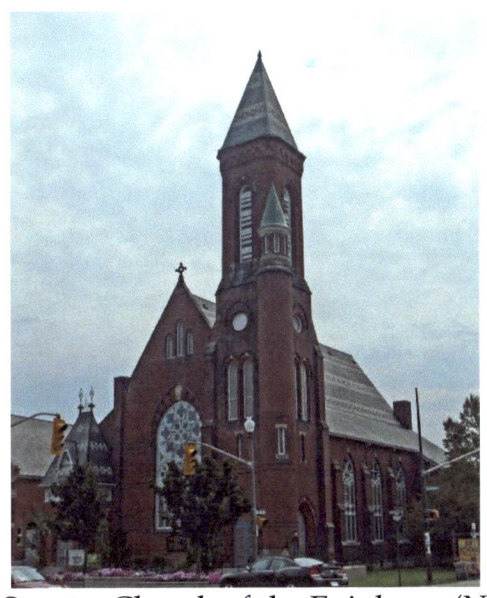

560 Dundas Street – Church of the Epiphany (New St. Paul's Anglican Church) was built at the intersection of Wellington and Dundas Streets – opened in 1879 to accommodate the growing congregation – buttresses, rose window

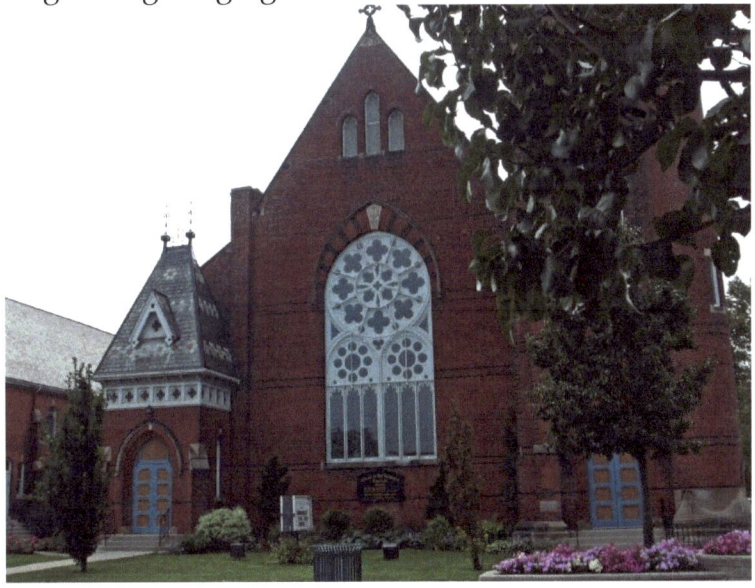

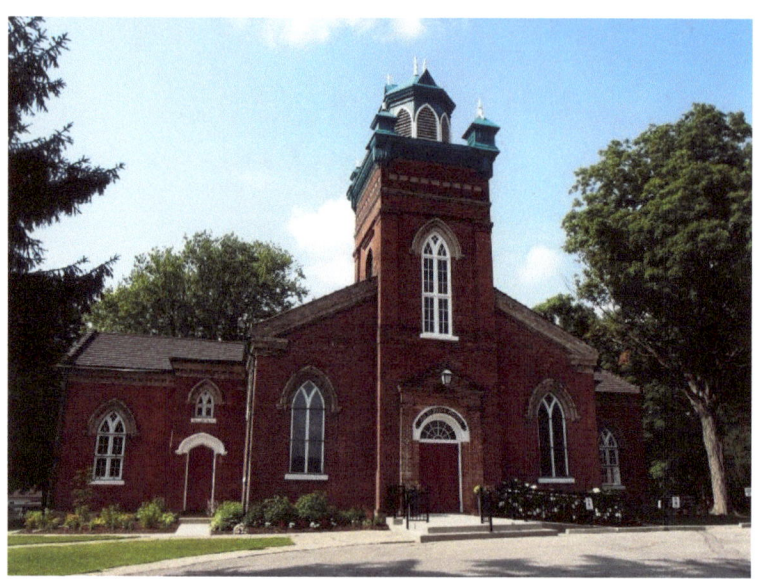

     723 Dundas Street – Old St. Paul's Church – 1834 - The red-brick church was designed in the Gothic Revival style – lancet windows, dichromatic brickwork. The front elevation has a classically-inspired cornice return, a semi-circular transom over the main entrance door with a brick pediment and pilasters. The tower has a hexagonal cupola with louvered, pointed-arch openings. The base of the cupola is decorated with a dentil trim and bracketed cornice. The low-pitched, timber-frame roof is an example of construction methods used during the 1830s.

     Old St. Paul's was closed in 1879 (when New St. Paul's opened) but re-opened to serve the Anglican community in 1882.

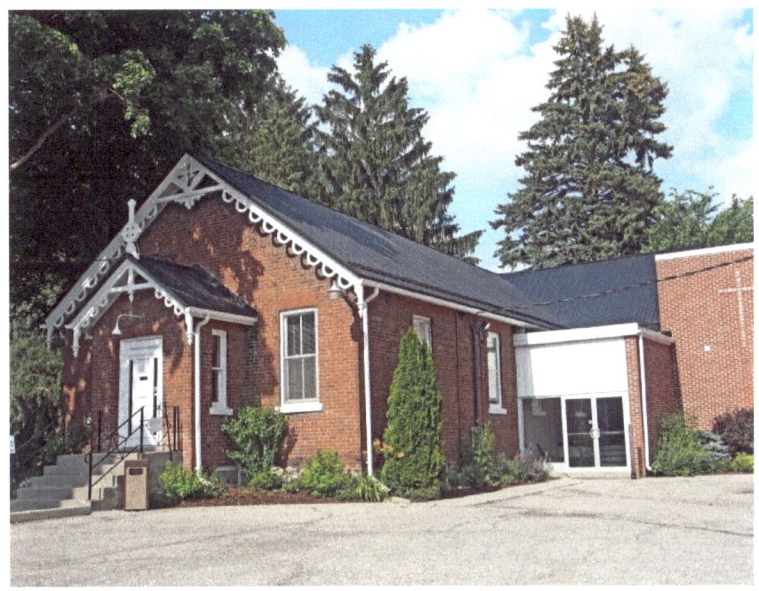

Verge board trim

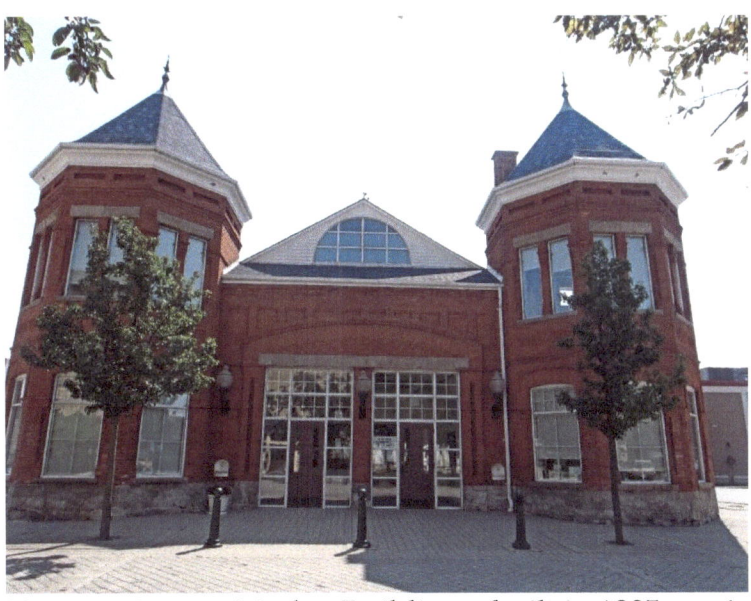

22 Reeve Street - Market Building – built in 1895 – twin
towers, use of stone in the trim

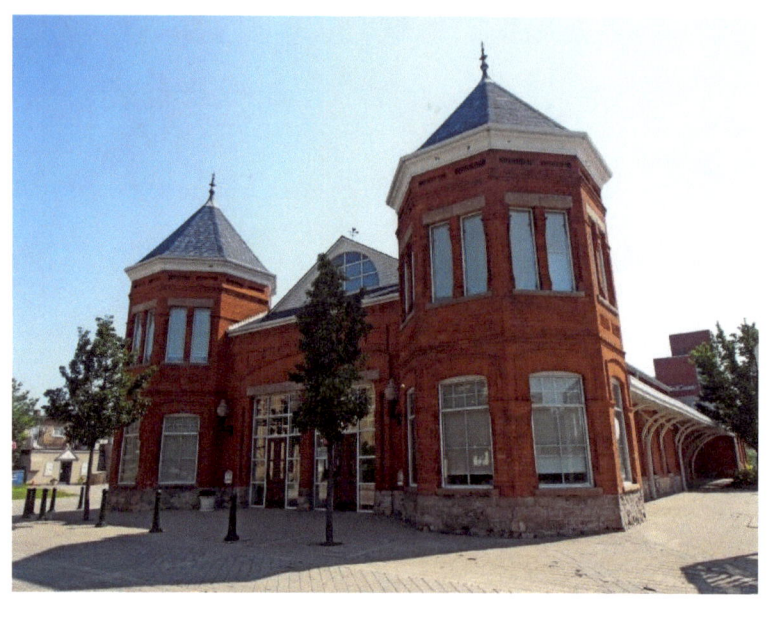

The Market Building

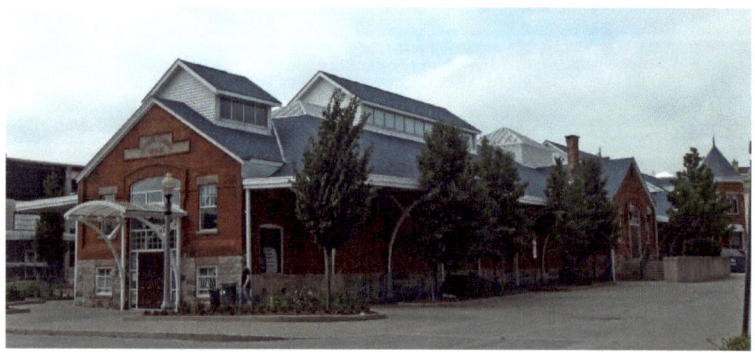

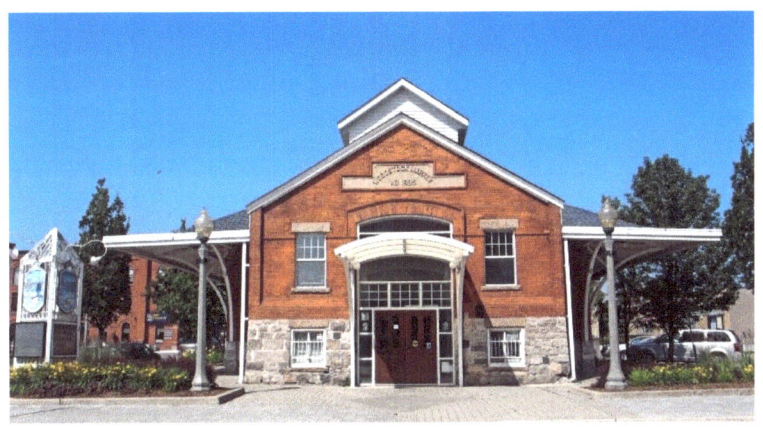

Market Building

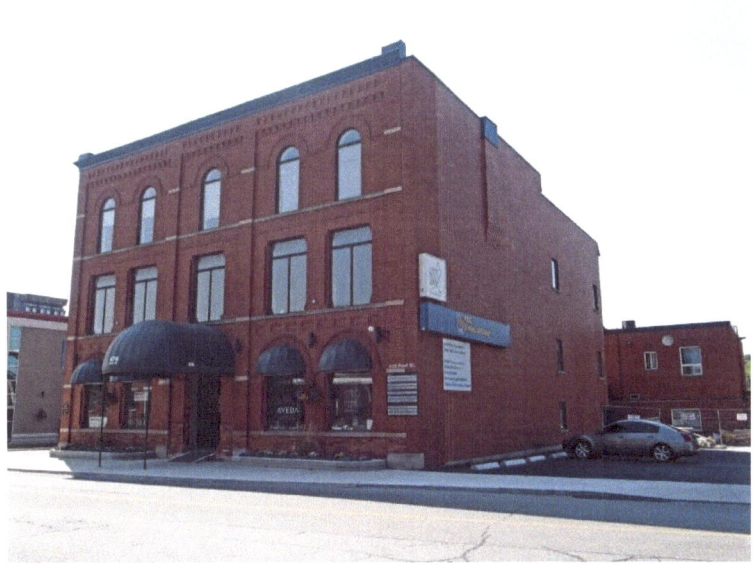

476 Peel Street – Edwardian style – 3 storey red brick, flat roof
– decorative brickwork, patterned cornice, drip mouldings
above the windows

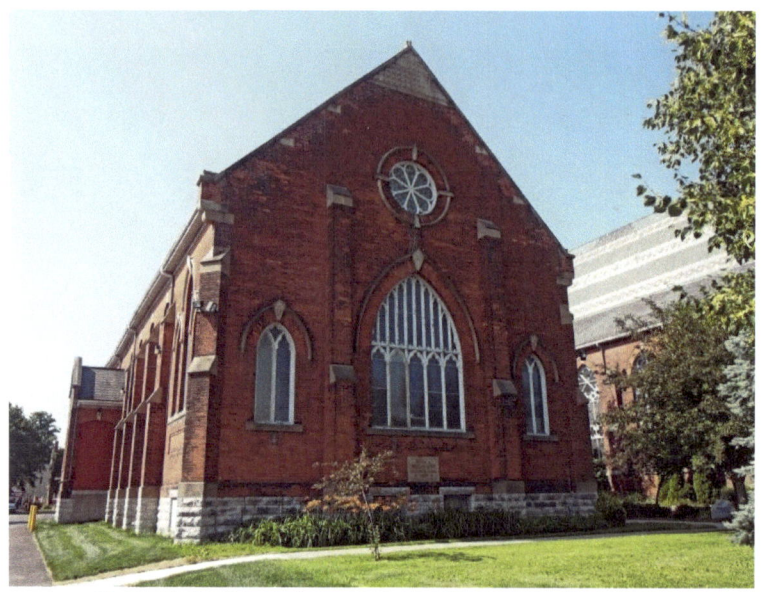

Rose window, buttresses, lancet windows

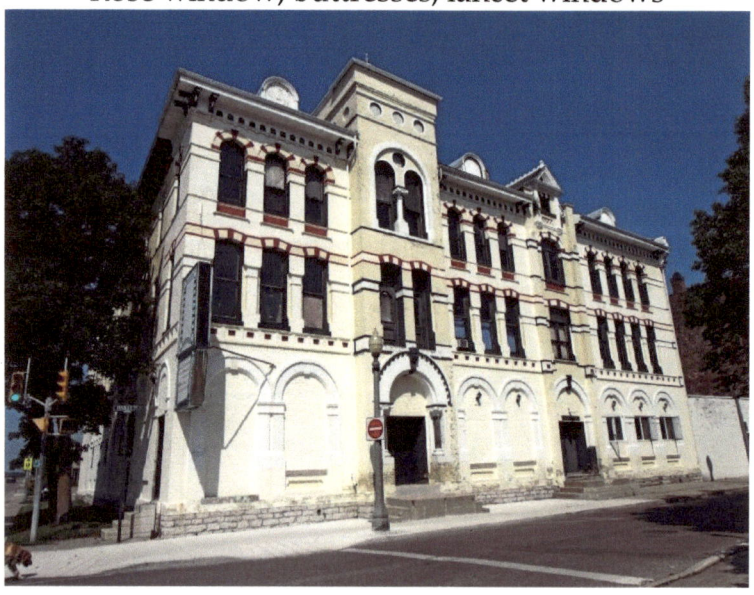

Finkle Street – The Oxford Hotel, located across from Market Square and the Town Hall in Woodstock was built in 1880 as "The O'Neill House" in Romanesque style. It saw guests such as Oscar Wilde and Reginald Birchall.

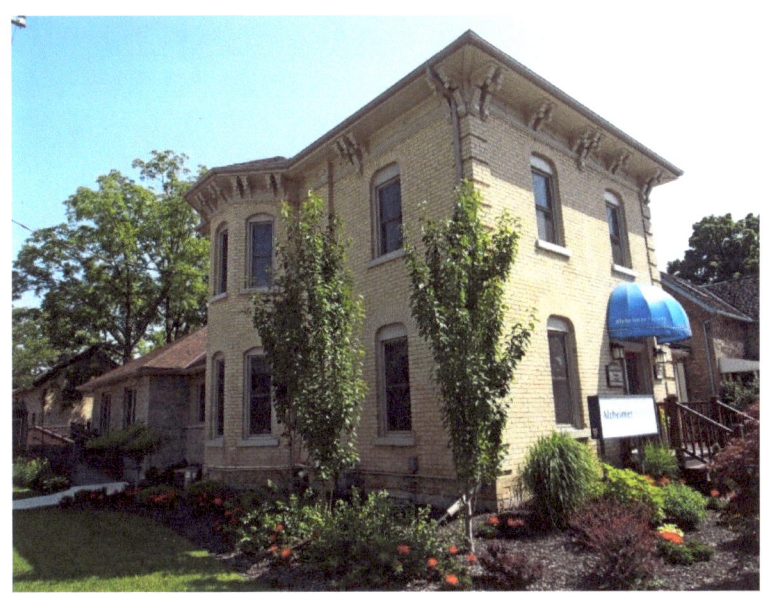

575 Victoria Street – Italianate – cornice brackets, corner quoins, two-storey bay window

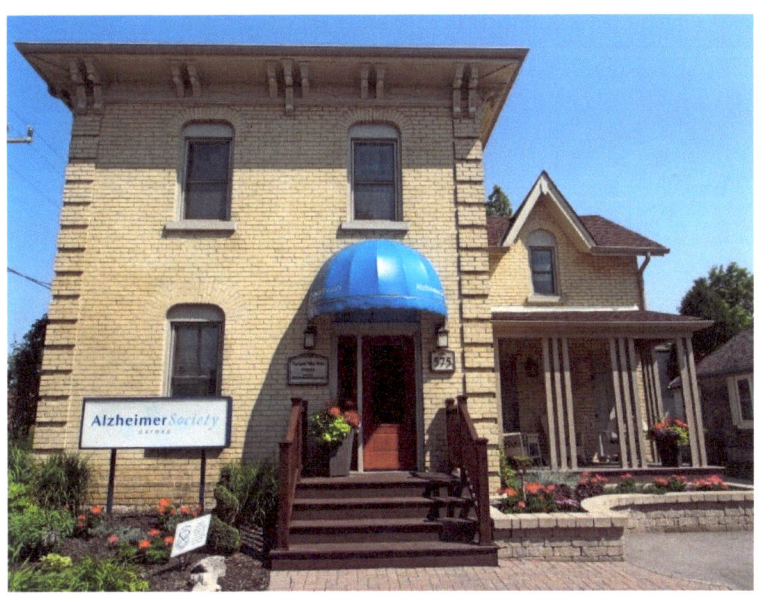

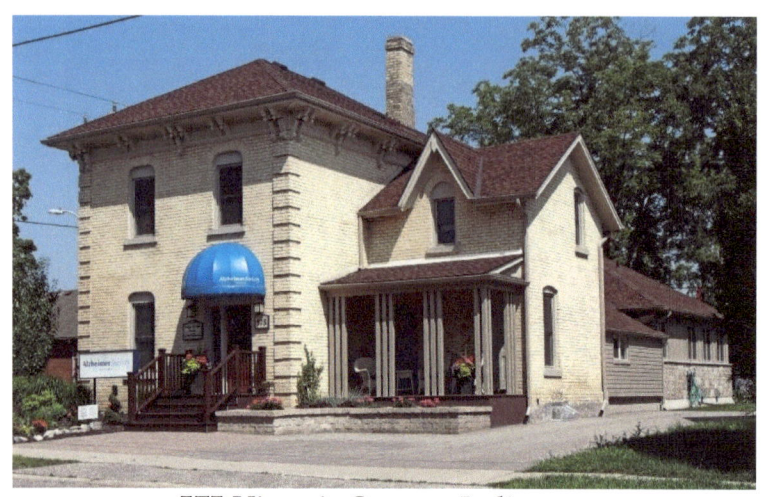

575 Victoria Street – Italianate
with Gothic addition on the right

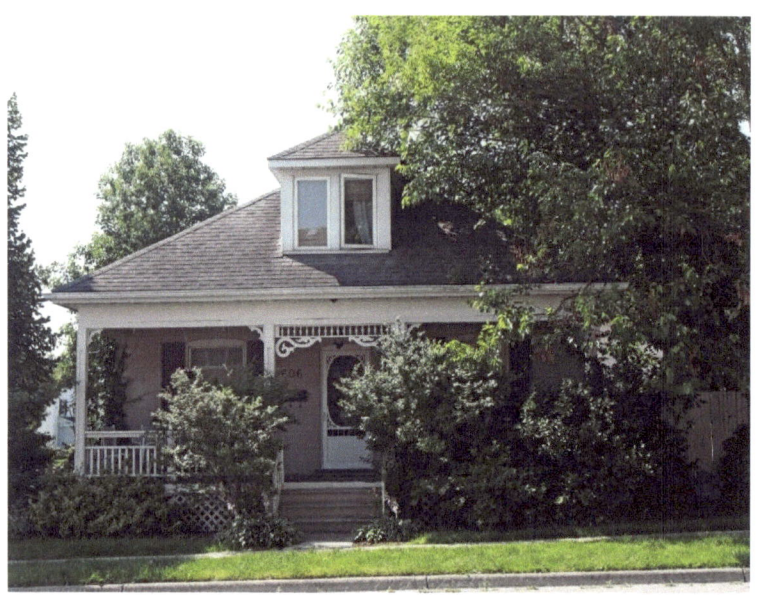

606 Victoria Street – Regency cottage with dormer in attic

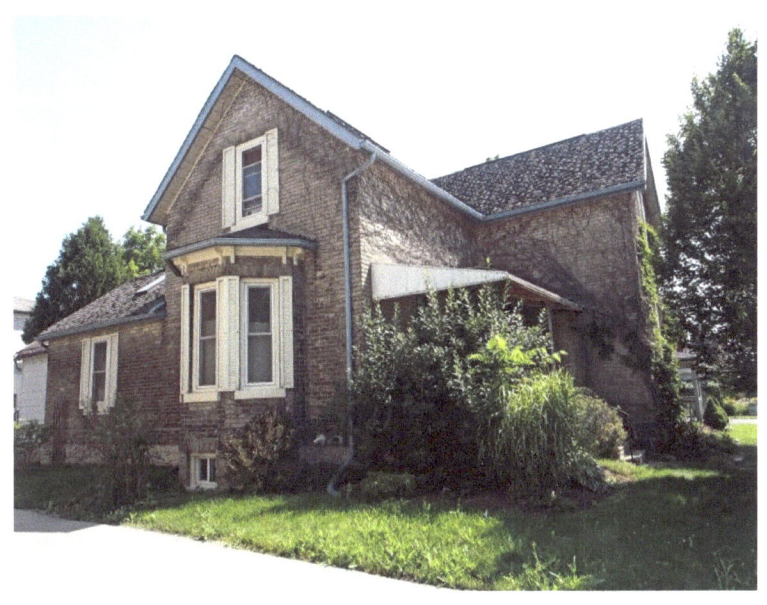

581 Victoria Street – cobblestone, bay window

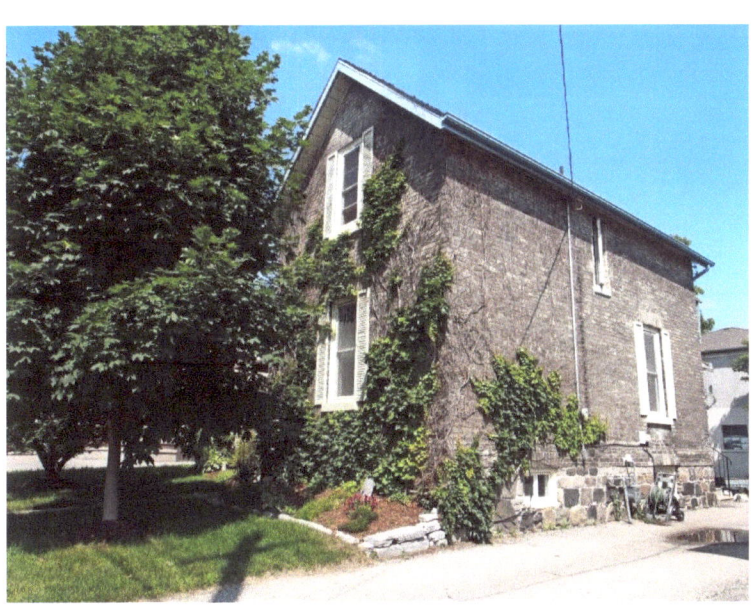

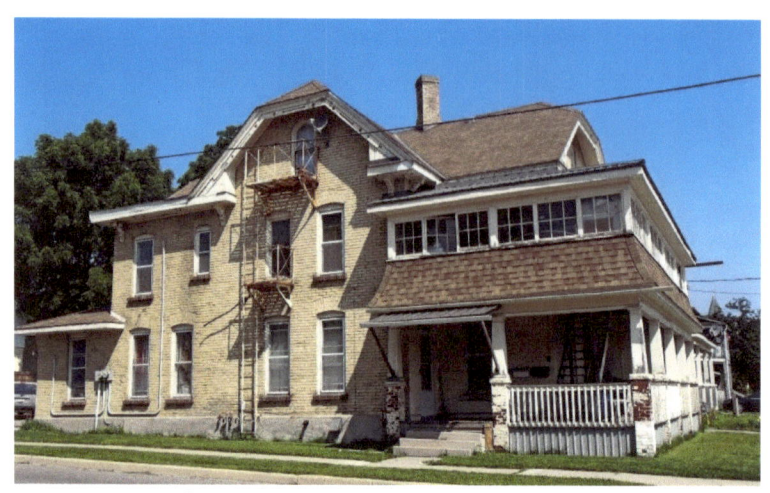

24 Victoria Street - vernacular

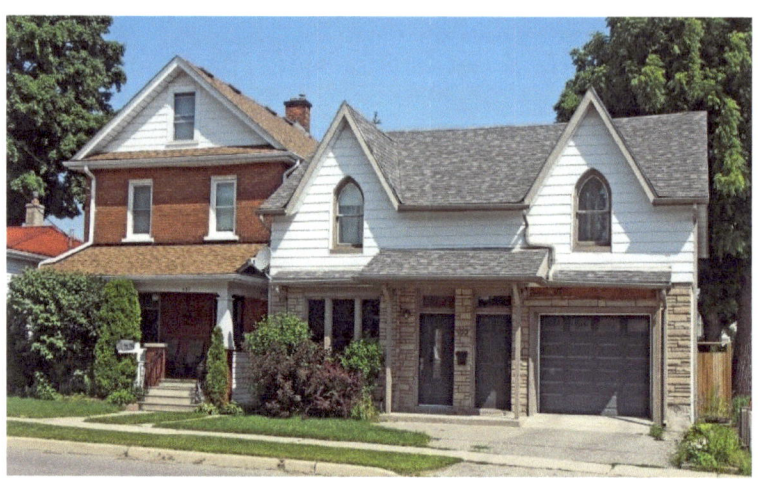

599 Victoria Street - Edwardian

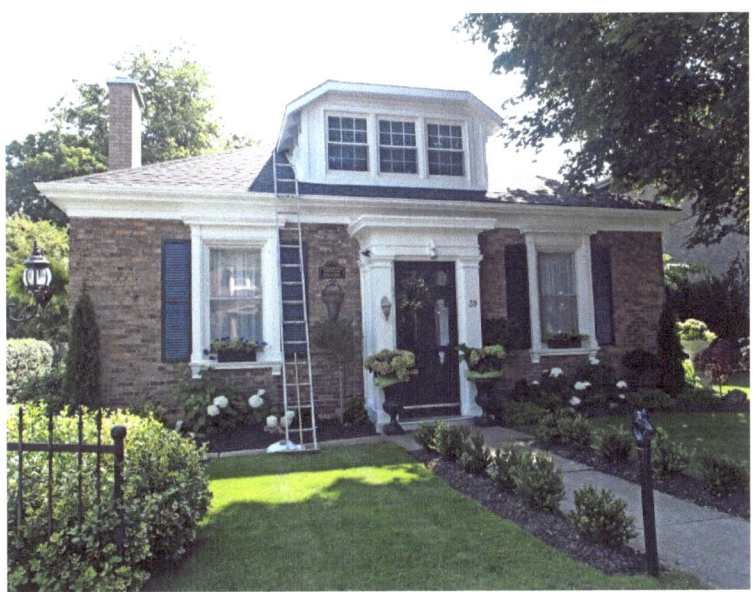

39 Victoria Street – Neo-Classical cottage is a 1½ storey buff brick home, hip roof, centred dormer; windows have wooden lintels and brackets supporting the sills; three panel double door on the storm porch has an interesting window shape in the door; field stone foundation

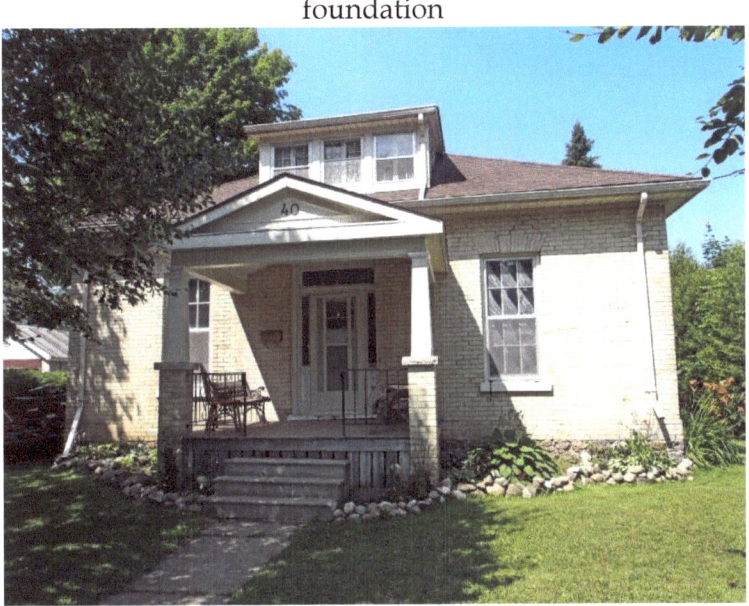

40 Victoria Street – pediment, dormer

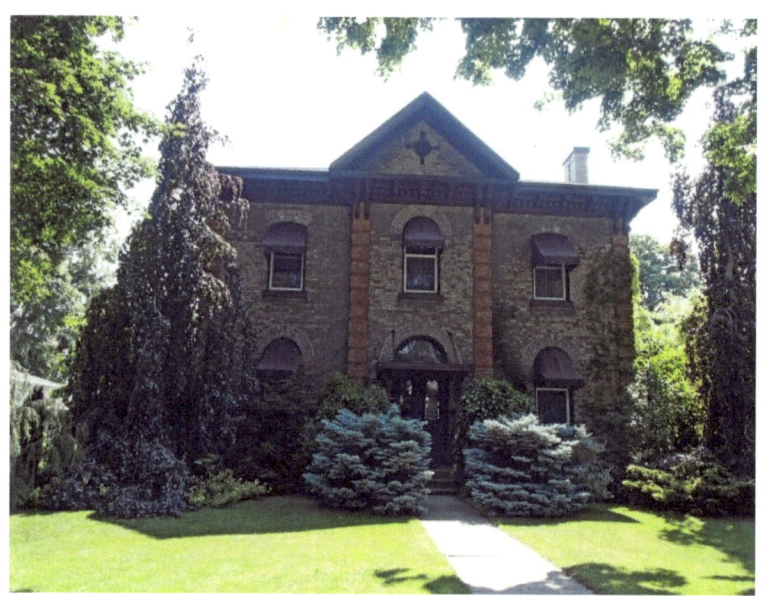

45 Victoria Street – Italianate, two-storey buff brick with red brick quoins, trunked hip roof with Neo-Classical pediment above the front entrance; wide cornice with small brackets ending with larger paired brackets at the corners

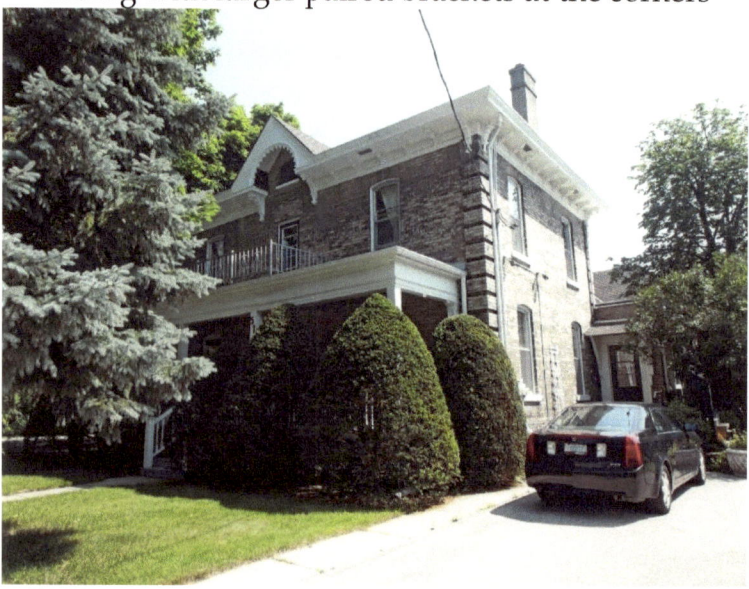

51 Victoria Street – corner quoins, cornice brackets

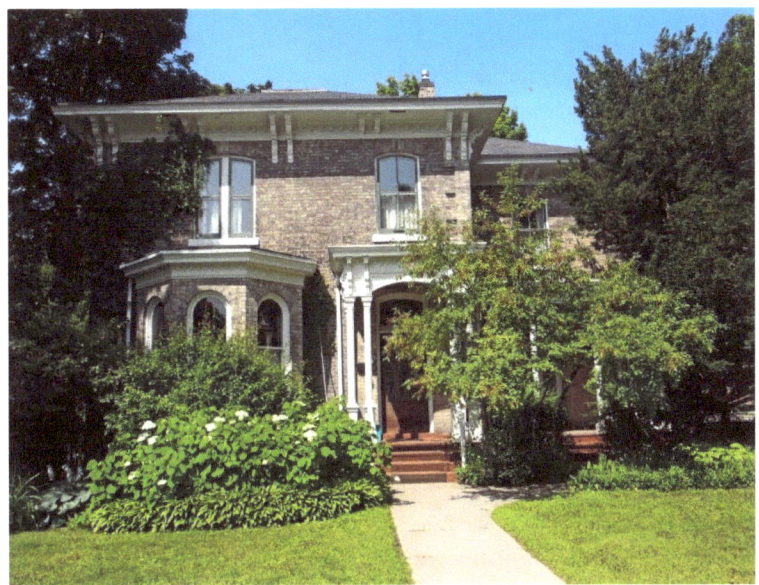

52 Victoria Street South – Italianate, full two-storey, buff brick, quoins, trunked hip roof with wide cornice, dentils, and small paired brackets between larger paired brackets; open porch with paired turned posts on wooden pedestals; ellipse-shaped transom above door

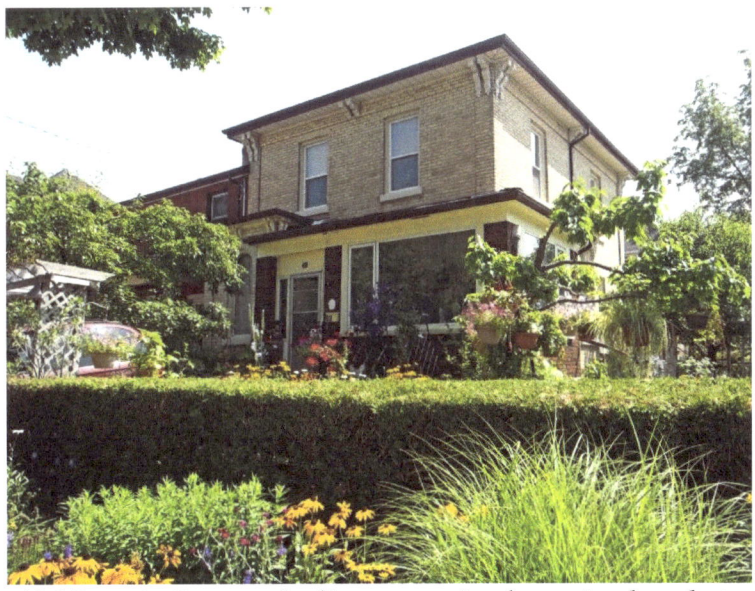

69 Victoria Street – Italianate, paired cornice brackets

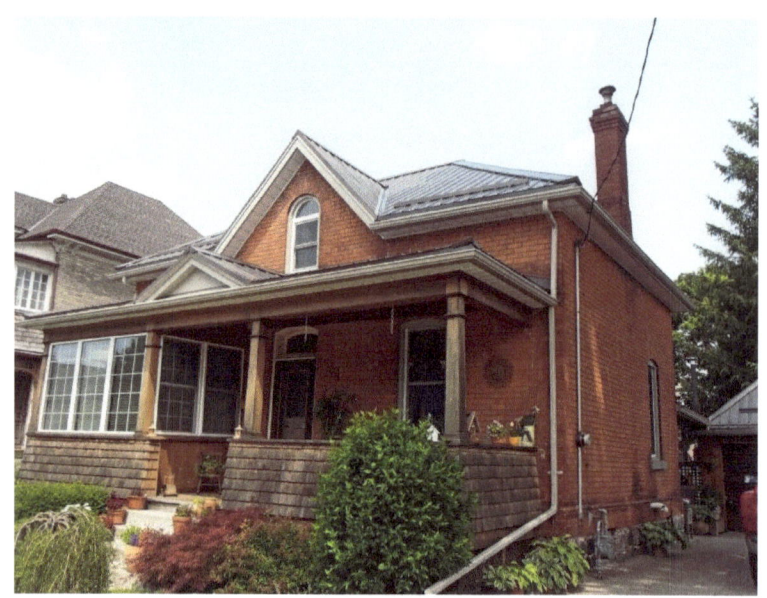

521 Grace Street

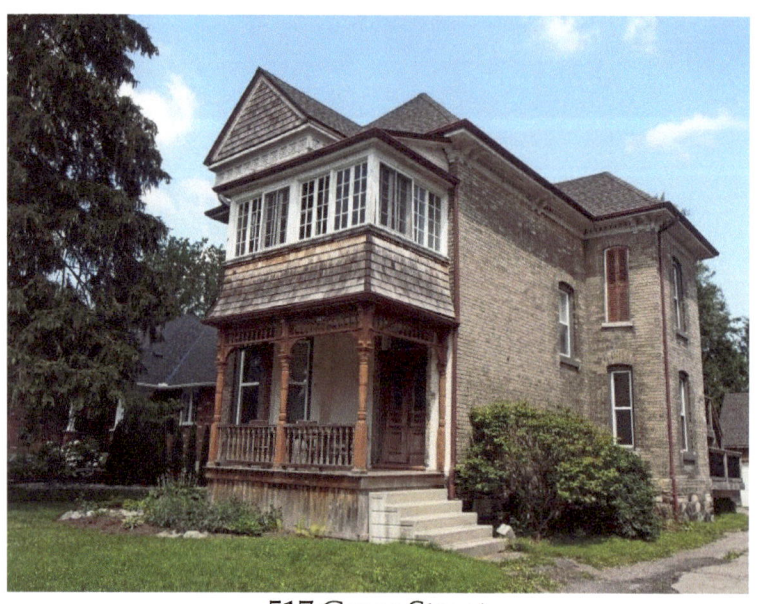

517 Grace Street

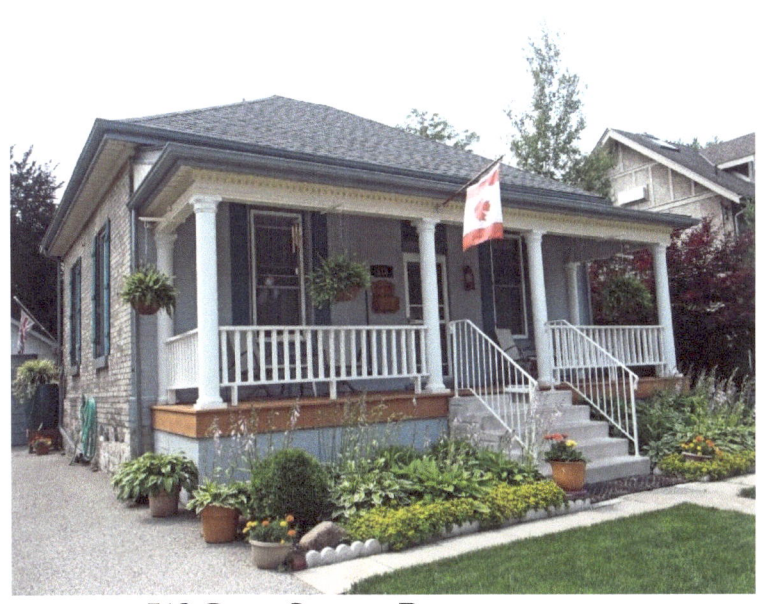
518 Grace Street – Regency cottage

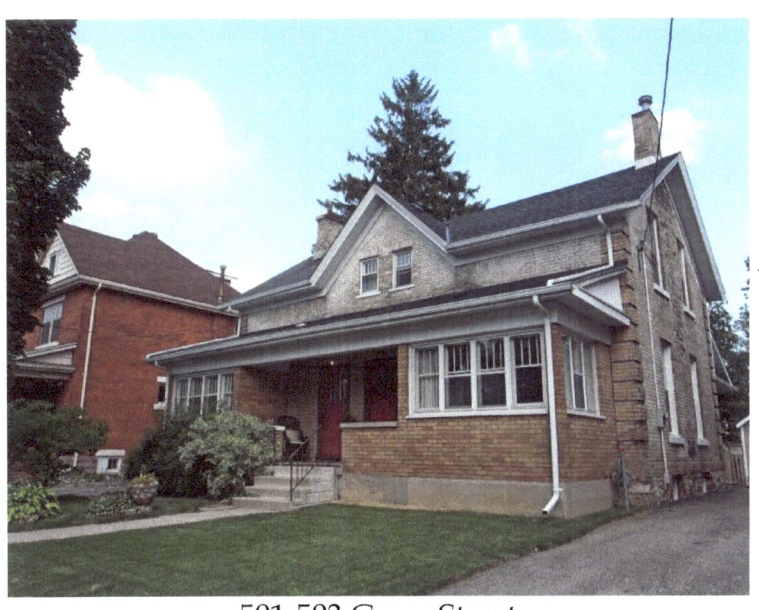
501-503 Grace Street

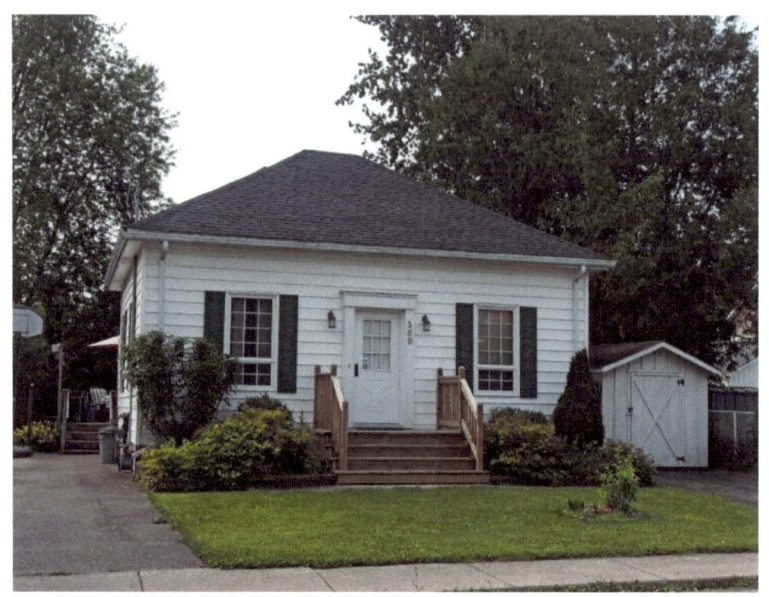

500 Grace Street – Regency cottage

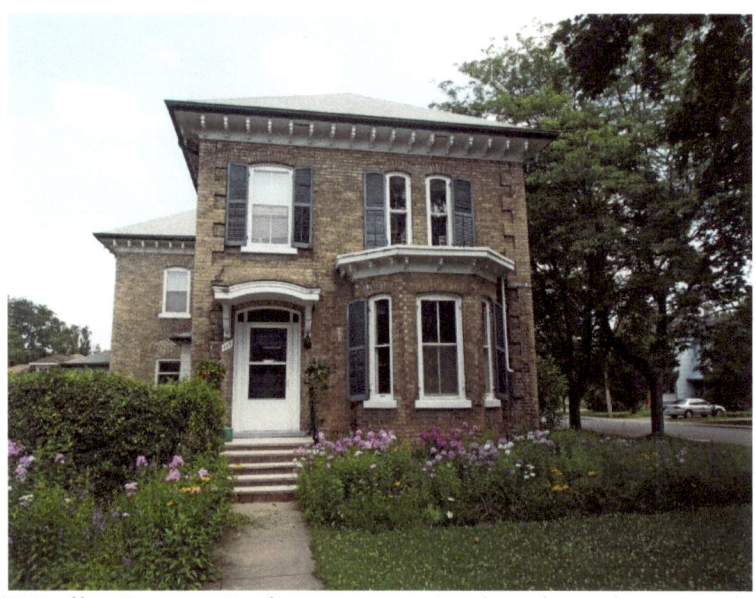

467 Buller Street – Italianate, cornice brackets, bay window

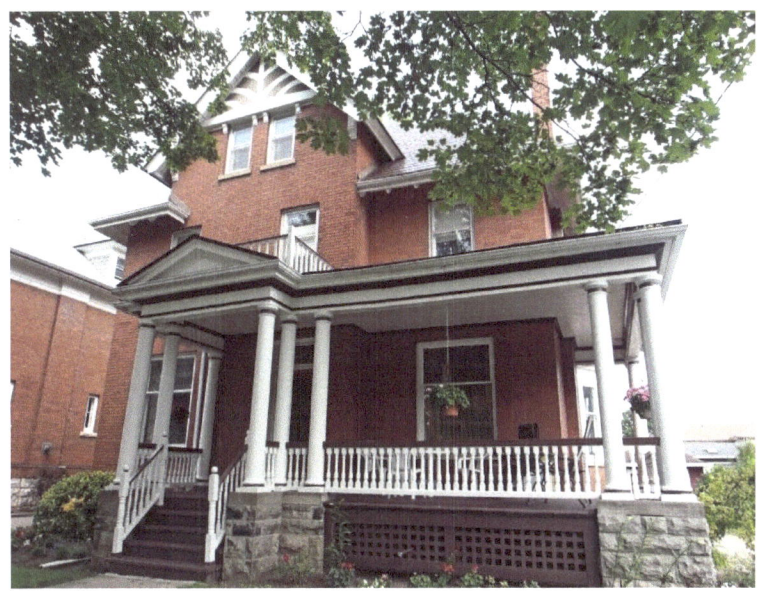

463 Buller Street – pediment, wraparound verandah

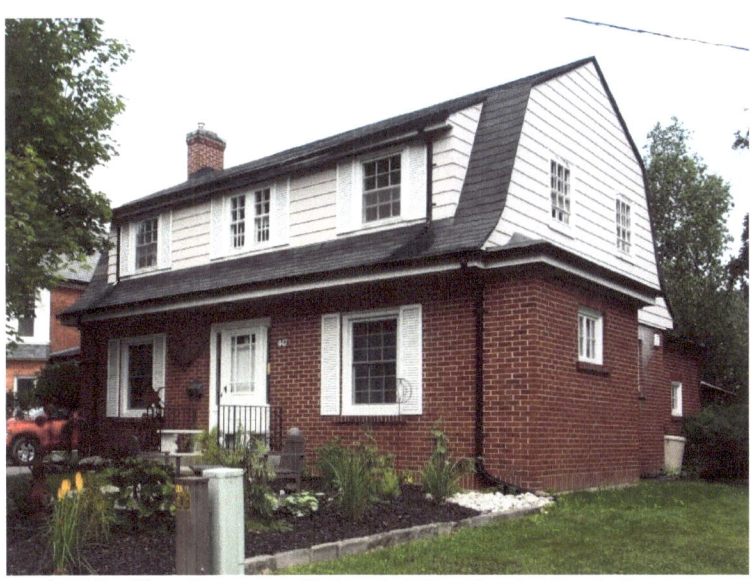

447 Buller Street – Colonial Revival, shed dormer

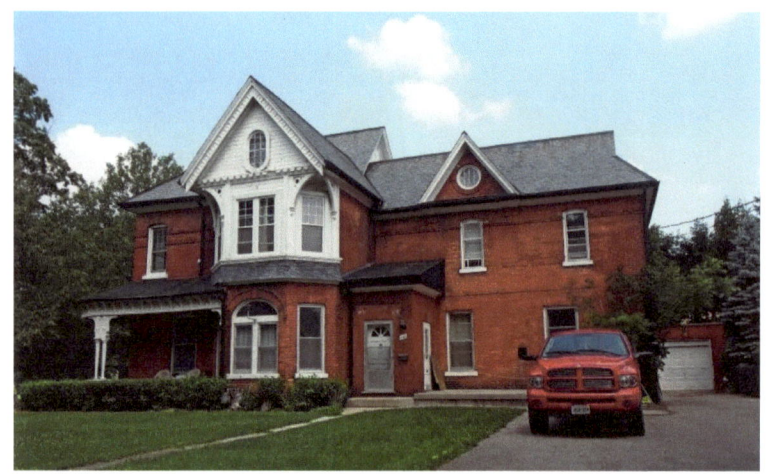

445 Buller Street – fretwork, oval window in main gable, round window in small gable

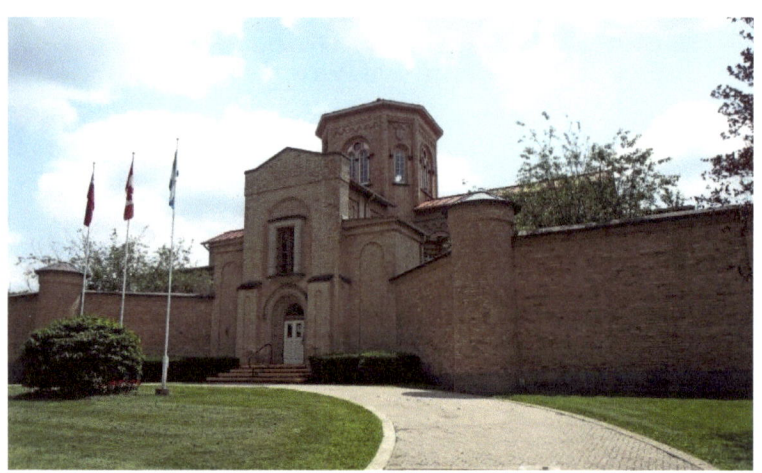

410 Buller Street – James Hay residence "Eastdene"– 1878 – industrialist born in Woodstock, one of founders of Board of Trade in 1878; served on Town Council – now occupied by Oxford County Public Health

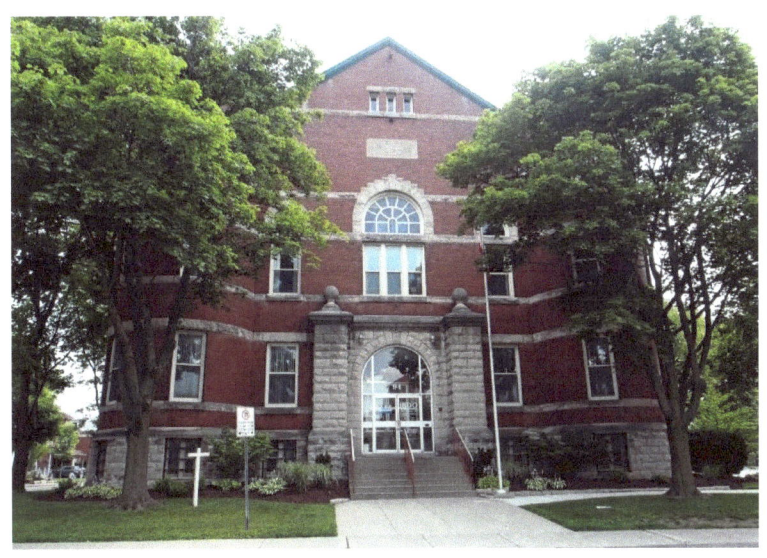

94 Graham Street – Woodstock Armoury - 1904

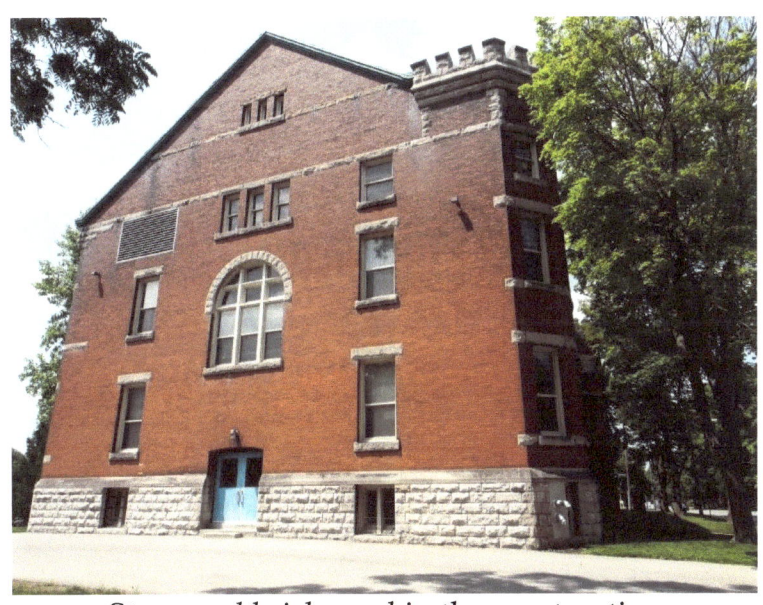

Stone and brick used in the construction

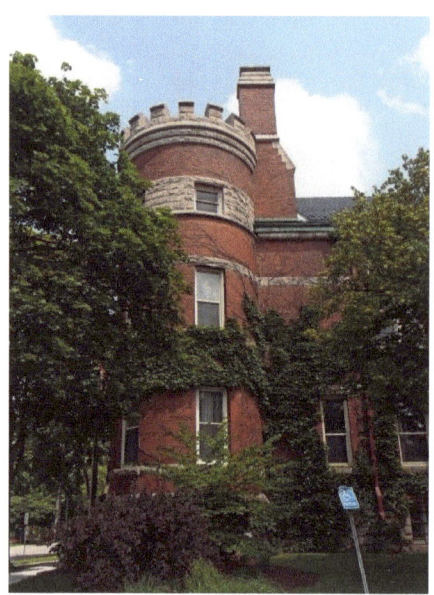

Crenelated tower

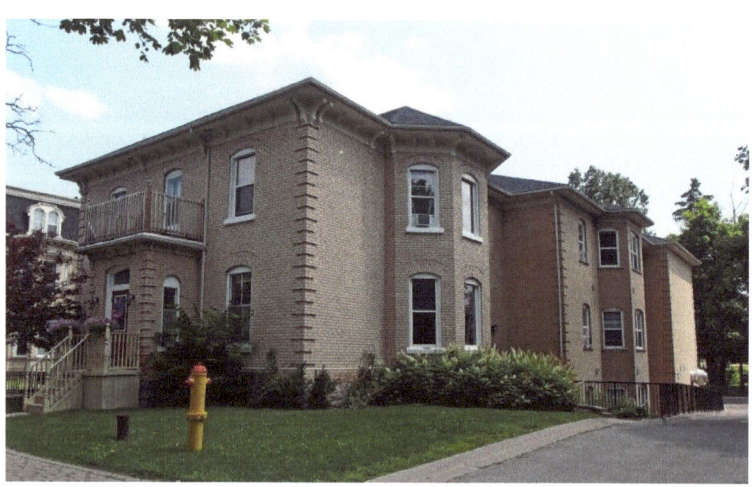

Graham Street – corner quoin, cornice brackets

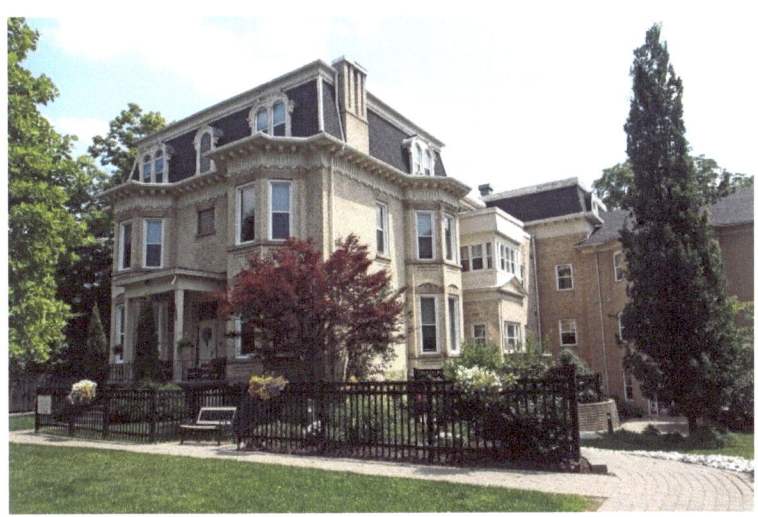

126 Graham Street – Park Place Retirement Centre
Second Empire style – mansard roof, window hoods,
decorative cornice

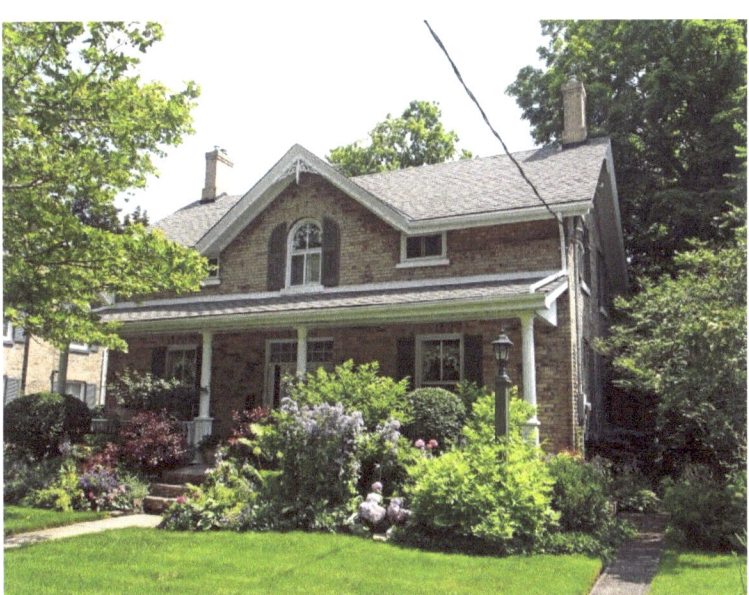

136 Graham Street – Gothic Revival, verge board trim on
gable, sidelights and transom around front door

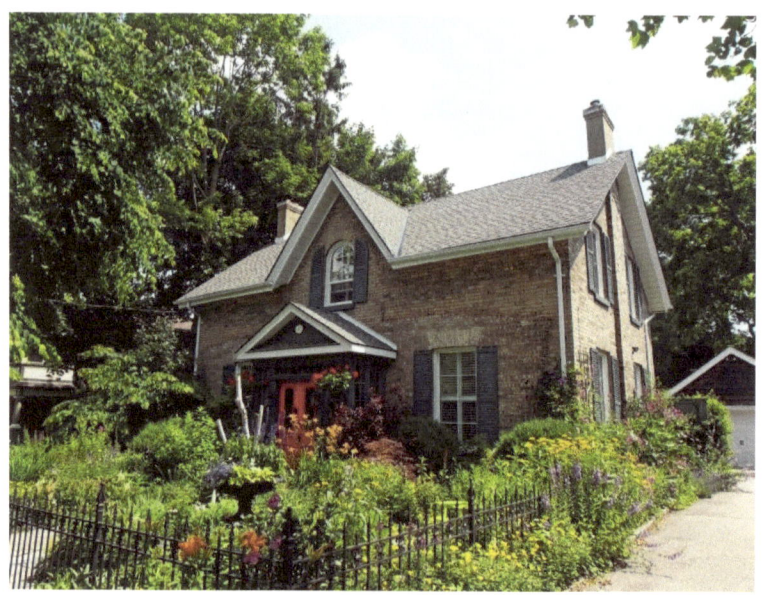

140 Graham Street – Gothic Revival - pediment

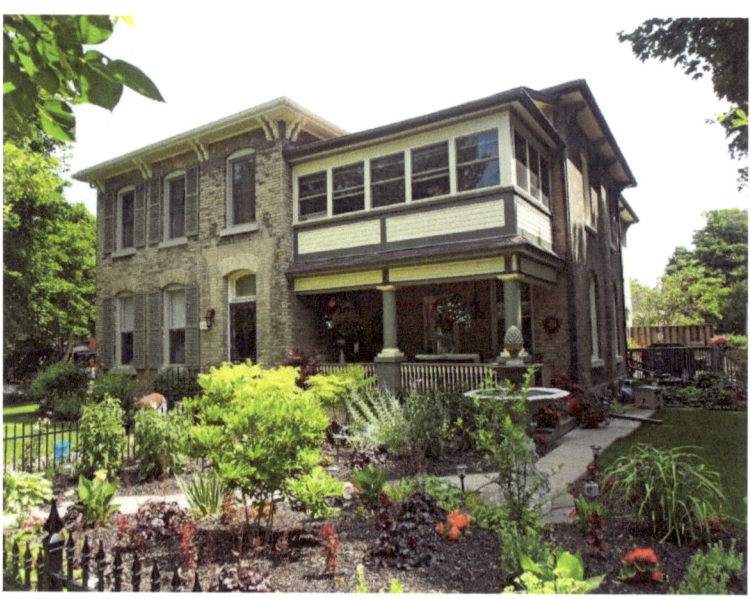

148 Graham Street – Italianate, paired cornice brackets,
enclosed upper balcony

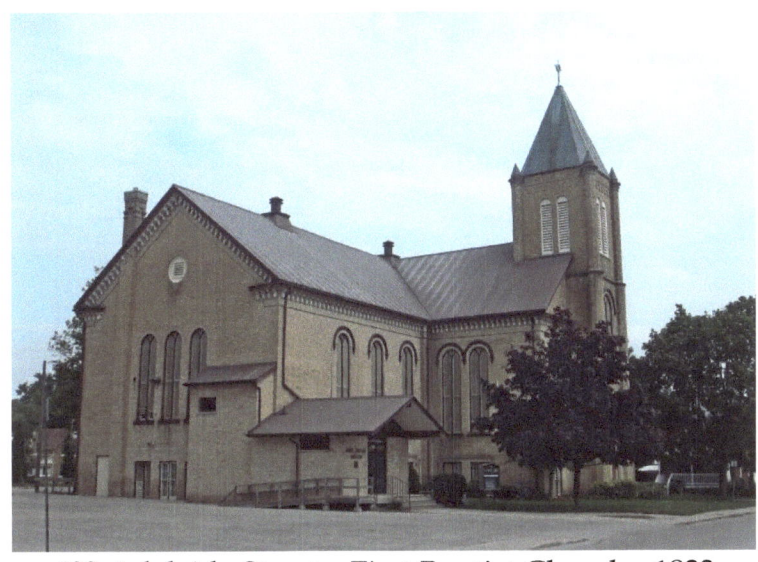

603 Adelaide Street – First Baptist Church - 1822

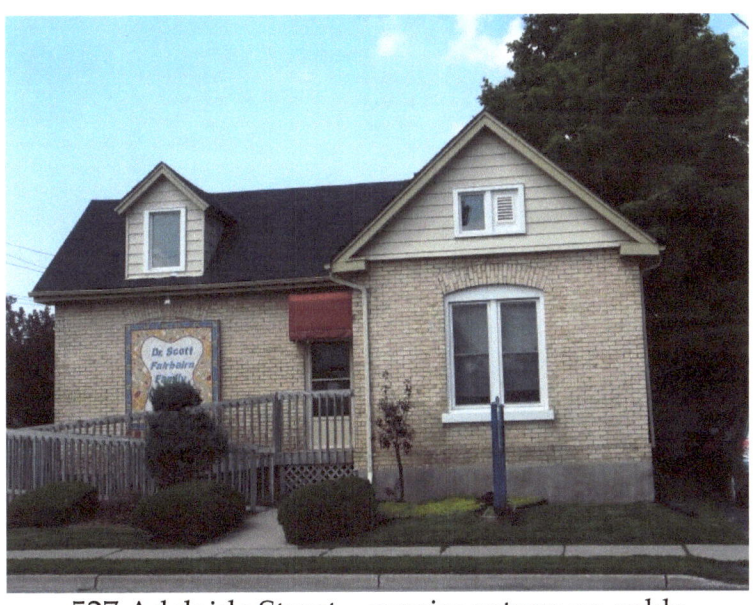

527 Adelaide Street – cornice return on gable

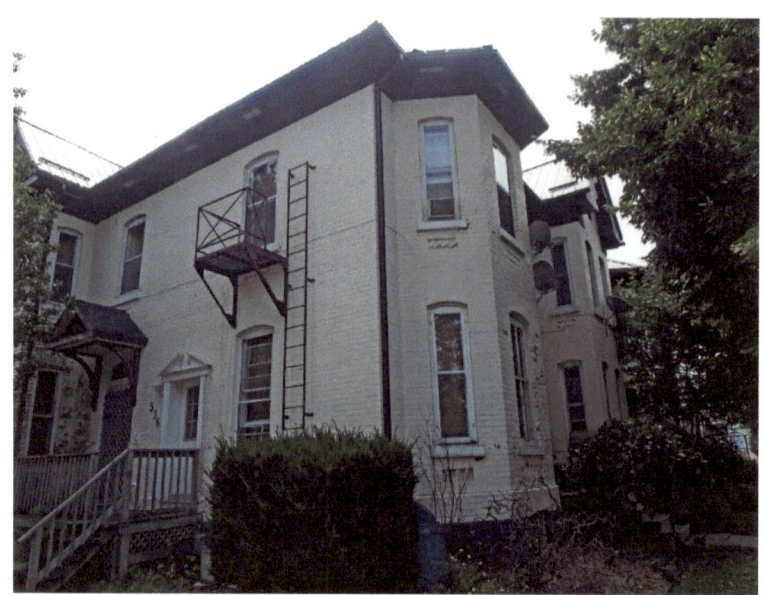

536 Adelaide Street

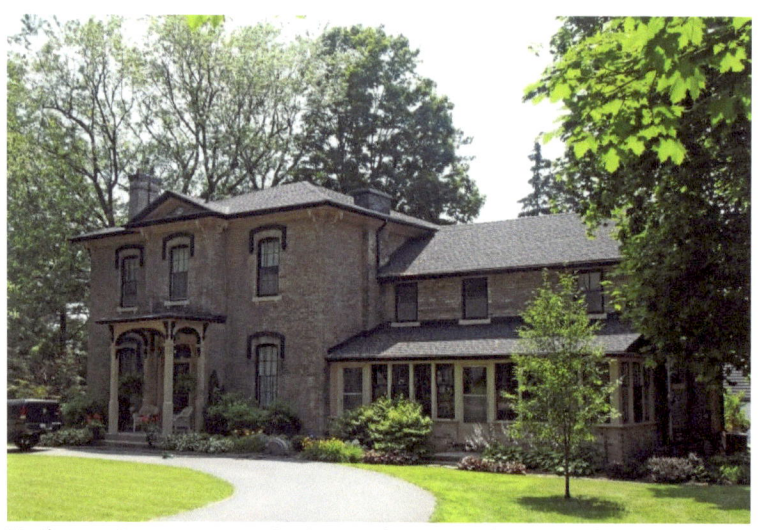

145 Delatre Street – c. 1846 – Italianate, hip roof, entrance, drip moulding over windows in two-storey section, pediment, cornice brackets; enclosed verandah on 1½ storey section

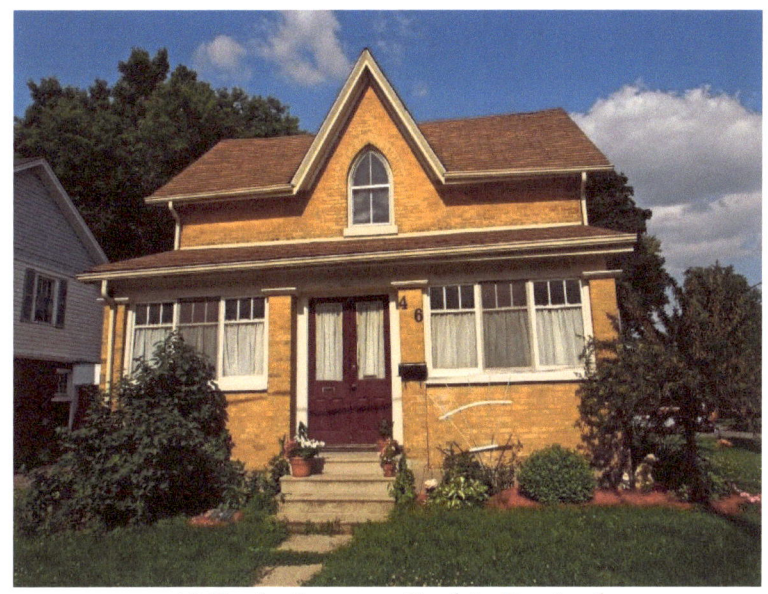

46 Beale Street – Gothic Revival

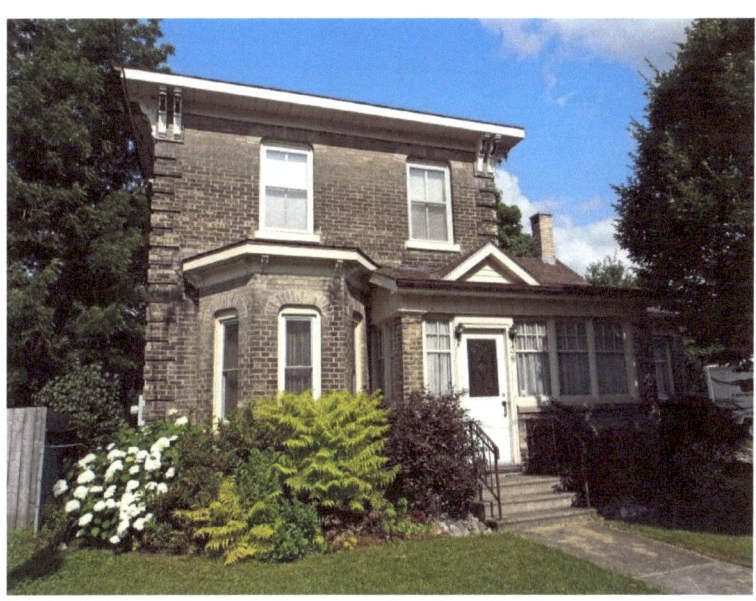

36 Beale Street – Italianate, cornice brackets, corner quoin, bay window, pediment above enclosed porch

Architectural Terms

Banding: Different materials, colors or textures used in horizontal bands along a wall. Example: 365 Dundas Street, Page 21	
Bay Window: A window that projects out from a wall, in a semicircular, rectangular, or polygonal design. Used frequently in Gothic and Victorian designs. Example: 581 Victoria Street, Page 39	
Brackets: a decorative or weight-bearing structural element which forms a right angle with one side against a wall and the other under a projecting surface such as an eave or roof. Example: 73 Wilson Street, Page 7	
Buttress: a masonry structure built against or projecting from a wall which serves to support or reinforce the wall. In Canadian architecture, they are sometimes used for decoration. Example: 285 Dundas Street, Page 26	

Cobblestone architecture: Refers to the use of cobblestones embedded in mortar as a method for erecting walls on houses and commercial buildings. Example: 22 Wilson Street, Page 9	
Cornice: originally the wooden overhang of the roof. With the use of stone, brick, iron and steel, the cornice is any projecting shelf at the top of a ceiling or roof. They can be very decorative. Example: 476 Dundas Street, Page 14	
Cornice Return: decorative element on the end of a gable. Example: 527 Adelaide Street, Page 53	
Cupola: A domed or curved roof rising from a building as a decorative element. Example: 723 Dundas Street, Page 32	
Dentil Moulding: an even series of rectangles used as ornamental decoration in cornices. Example: 521 Dundas Street, Page 10	

Dichromatic brickwork: the use of two colours of brick, tile or slate to decorate a façade. Example: 433 Dundas Street, Page 17	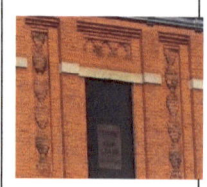
Dormer: (French for "sleep") a gable end window that pierces through the plane of a sloping roof surface to create usable space in the top floor or attic of a building by adding headroom. Example: 39 Victoria Street, Page 41	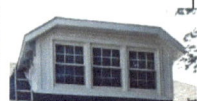
Entrance: The entrance encompasses the doorway and the inner vestibule or, in residential architecture, the covered porch. Example: 145 Delatre Street, Page 54	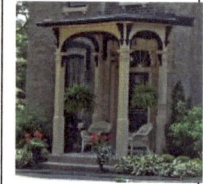
Fretwork: interlaced decorative design resembling a bracket Example: 445 Buller Street, Page 48	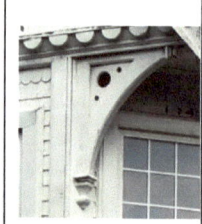
Gable: the triangular portion of a wall between the edges of a sloping roof. **Jacobean Gable:** the gable extends above the roofline. Example: 581 Victoria Street, Page 39	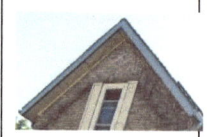

Hipped Roof: a roof where all sides slope downwards to the walls with no gables. Example: 50-52 Wilson Street, Page 7	
Keystones and Voussoirs: a voussoir is a wedge-shaped element used in building an arch. A keystone is the central stone that locks all the stones into position, allowing the arch to bear weight. A keystone is often enlarged and embellished. Example: 425 Dundas Street, Pg.18	
Lancet Window: a tall, narrow window with a pointed arch at its top. Example: 723 Dundas Street, Page 32	
Mansard Roof: This style was popularized by Francois Mansart (1598-1666), an accomplished architect of the French Baroque period and especially fashionable during the Second French Empire (1852-1870). This roof is almost flat on the top section, with two slopes on each of its sides with the lower slope at a steeper angle than the upper and having dormer windows. Example: 136 Graham Street, Page 51	
Pediment: a triangular section above the horizontal structure (entablature), typically supported by columns. The inside of the triangle is called the tympanum. Example: 419 Dundas Street, Page 18	

Pilaster: a slightly projecting column built into or applied to the face of a wall for additional structural support. Example: 521 Dundas Street, Page 10	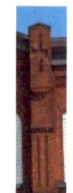
Quoin: masonry blocks at the corner of a wall, often a decorative feature, usually larger or of a different colour than the rest of the wall. Example: 575 Victoria Street, Page 37	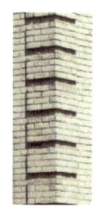
Rose Window: a circular window with ornamental tracery radiating from the centre. Example: Dundas Street, Page 36	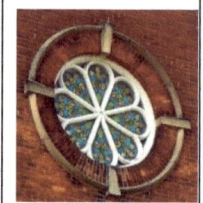
Sidelight: a window, usually with a vertical emphasis, that flanks a door, and is often used to emphasize the importance of a primary entrance. **Transom Window:** the light above the doorway, also called a fanlight. Example: 136 Graham Street, Page 51	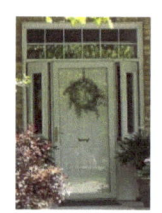

Turret: a small tower that projects from the wall of a building. Example: 51 Wilson Street, Page 10	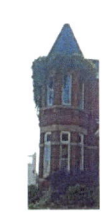
Verge board and Finial: also called bargeboards – hang from the projecting end of a roof and are often elaborately carved and ornamented. **Finial:** ornament added to the top of a gable, pinnacle, canopy or spire – a Gothic element. Example: 723 Dundas Street, Page 33	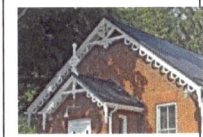
Window Hood: A **hood** is the piece found above window openings, usually of an ornate design, and covers the top third of the opening. Hoods are commonly placed above arched or curved openings on both windows and doors. Example: 425 Dundas Street, Page 18	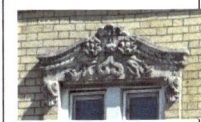

Edwardian, 1900-1930 – This style bridges the ornate and elaborate styles of the Victorian era and the simplified styles of the 20th century. Balanced facades, simple roof lines, dormer windows, large front porches, and smooth brick surfaces are its characteristics. Example: 476 Peel Street, Page 35	
Gothic Revival, 1830-1890 – These decorative buildings have sharply-pitched gables with highly detailed verge boards, pointed-arch window openings, and dichromatic brickwork. It is a common style in Ontario. Example: 46 Beale Street	
Italianate, 1850-1900 – It has wide-bracketed eaves, belvederes, wrap-around verandahs. Example: 467 Buller Street, Page 55	
Neo-Classical (1810 - 1850) – This style was a direct result of the War of 1812. Many Upper Canadians returning from the war with the United States were second or third generation Loyalists who had inherited land and means from their forefathers. Once the conflict had passed, they had the money and the time to expand their holdings and indulge their architectural whims. Both residential and commercial buildings were constructed on the traditional Georgian plan, but they had a new gaiety and light-heartedness. Detailing became more refined, delicate, and elegant. Example: 39 Victoria Street, Page 41	

Neocolonial (also Colonial Revival, Georgian Revival or Neo-Georgian) architecture seeks to revive elements of architectural style of American colonial architecture of the period around the Revolutionary War which drew strongly from Georgian architecture of Great Britain. Architecture from the 18th and early 19th centuries in Ontario includes a wide assortment of detailing and ornament applied to a design centered around the fireplace and the source of water. Structures are typically two stories, have a symmetrical front facade with elaborate front doorways, often with decorative crown pediments, fanlights, and sidelights, symmetrical windows flanking the front entrance, often in pairs or threes, and columned porches. Example: 447 Buller Street, Page 47	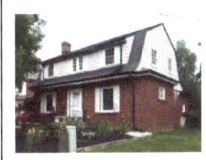
Regency Cottage, 1830-1860 – This style originated in England in 1815 and spread to Ontario later in the 19th century as British officers retired to Canada. It is a modest one-storey house with a low-pitched hip roof and has a symmetrical front façade. Example: 518 Grace Street, Page 45	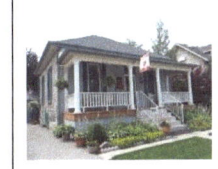
Romanesque Revival, 1880-1910 – This style hearkens back to medieval architecture of the 11th and 12th centuries with a heavy appearance, blocky towers and rounded arches. Example: 395 Dundas Street, Page 20	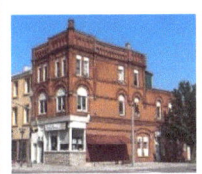

Second Empire, 1860-1880 – The mansard roof is the most noteworthy feature of this style and is evidence of the French origins. Projecting central towers and one or two-storey bays can also be present. Example: 350 Dundas Street, Page 21	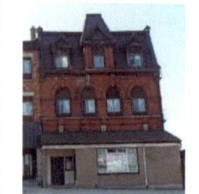
Vernacular/Traditional Mode 1638 - 1950 Influenced but not defined by a particular style, vernacular buildings are made from easily available materials and exhibit local design characteristics. Example: 24 Victoria Street, Page 40	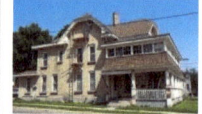

www.ingramcontent.com/pod-product-compliance
Lightning Source LLC
Chambersburg PA
CBHW040846180526
45159CB00001B/328